THE MEDITERRANEAN
SLOW COOKER COOKBOOK

The Mediterranean Slow Cooker Cookbook

50

Easy and Delicious Mediterranean Slow Cooker Recipes for Your Busy Life

Julia Garcia

Contents

Introduction

The Mediterranean cuisine is a wonderful mixture of so many significant cultural and regional differences between the Western Mediterranean, Southern Europe, and North Africa. It is, without a doubt, the richest cuisine in the world. Each region around the coast of the Mediterranean Sea gives a part of its long culinary tradition and a whole new flavor to this uniquely diverse diet. However, it is important to point out that some regions go deep in the land and are not a part of the Mediterranean shores, but their cultural background and history along with the food belong to this region.

Culinary tradition of Greece, Turkey, Syria, Lebanon, Palestine, Israel and Egypt belongs to the Eastern Mediterranean region. Foods like Feta cheese or Greek yogurt are almost always served with a meal and often followed with spices like parsley, rosemary, and mint. Lemon juice is a traditional substitute for vinegar in different vegetable combinations, while chickpeas serve as a perfect replacement for meat. Probably the most famous meals from this region are kebab, meatballs, and gyros. People are so creative in preparing these delicacies that you can easily say that every household has its own favorite recipe.

Southern European cuisine is a mixture of French, Italian, Spanish and Balkan cuisine. These beautiful dishes are often based on tomatoes, garlic, capers, anchovies, and mustard; usually combined into some mind-blowing meals. Pasta, rice, and other grains are the foundation of every meal, which is probably the most typical characteristic of this region. Southern Europe, however, has certain ingredients that are not traditional for other Mediterranean regions. Wine, for example, is often used for cooking to give extra flavor. But the tradition of wine goes even deeper and it is considered as the main component of a meal. A simple glass of wine is served with lunch or dinner to such an extent that every dish type has its own accompanying wine. In Spain, wine is often combined with different fresh and dried fruits, and served as a worldwide famous "sangria". The tradition is so strong that you can almost say that Spaniards don't consider sangria anymore as alcohol and even serve it to kids.

The North African part is the richest with spices. Morocco, Algeria, Tunisia, and Libya are countries known for cumin, coriander, saffron, cinnamon, cloves, chili and pepper. Just a pinch of these vibrant spices will make a perfect addition to stews, sauces, and soups. The North African region uses a massive amount of different dried fruits in so many different ways. Breakfast, warm and cold compotes, even dishes like roasted turkey, are unimaginable without a handful of raisins, prunes, dried figs, and dates. The most authentic meals of this region are often prepared in clay pots, over an open fire, and cooked for 12-24 hours, which probably makes them the best option for the original and authentic taste in your slow cooker.

The main reason why this area is so wonderfully rich in so many different meals is a moderate climate and a fertile soil. Sunny and relatively balanced climate contributed to the amazing agricultural growth. Even in ancient times, people recognized the Mediterranean region as the best place for life and cultural development. The unique position of the region makes it a crossroad between Europe, Africa, and Asia. This automatically made the Mediterranean region the biggest world's trading center, which of course affected the entire lifestyle and eating habits. Merchants from all over the world were coming to these regions to trade spices and other, mostly food, products. With all these new flavors coming from exotic India and later from the American continent, people learned some new ways of preparing their meals. The Mediterranean region, almost overnight, became a whole new "package of domestic ingredients with a pinch of other cultures to taste".

One of the most important symbols of the Mediterranean region and the most commonly used ingredient is definitely olive oil. Right after olive oil come vegetables like tomatoes, beans, onions, garlic, mushrooms, eggplants, and different types of leafy greens. Creative ways of preparing meals with these vegetables contribute to the immense richness of this cuisine, but the most common way of using them is the healthiest option – fresh in different salads that Mediterranean's love so much.

Meat, on the other hand, is used in small quantities, mostly for different grilled and stewed meals. However, dairy products are extremely popular. Just like in every other aspect, Mediterranean cuisine goes one step forward and forces you to choose the healthiest dairy option there is – sheep and goat's milk, cheese, and of course the famous yogurt. Most dishes are unimaginable without a good yogurt topping or a slice of soft goat's cheese.

Leaning on the shores of one of the richest seas in the world, Mediterranean regions use its full capacity. Various fish species and seafood are almost always on the menu in so many different and healthy ways, very often prepared with different herbs and spices which makes this cuisine so unique. The climate and geographic location are just perfect for herb and spices growth. Basil, oregano, rosemary, thyme, parsley, garlic, mint, dill, cilantro, saffron, and many others are exactly what gives the Mediterranean cuisine its specific warm and vibrant taste the world loves so much.

This cookbook includes long years of travel and studying local and authentic recipes of all three regions. A collection of 50 rich and diverse recipes perfectly suitable for your slow cooker which will please everyone at the table. From Morocco, Turkey, and Greece to Spain, Balkans, and France – this cookbook has it all covered. I hope these simple recipes will bring some healthy and tasty changes to your busy schedule and make you fall in love with the best cuisine this world has to offer – the Mediterranean cuisine!

CHAPTER ONE

The Benefits of Slow Cooking

One of the most important appliances in the Mediterranean cuisine is definitely a slow cooker. The reason is very simple – the entire traditional Mediterranean lifestyle, including the cuisine, is very slow. This is probably the biggest advantage of the Mediterranean cuisine. Slow cooking is proven to be the healthiest way of preparing your food. And not only that, we all have to agree that a food prepared like this is ten times tastier than any other cooking method. For the Mediterranean region, cooking has always been a ritual rather than a simple way to satisfy your need for energy. Slowly cooked tender meat pieces with different vegetables and spices are raised to a level of art and science, which is exactly why this cuisine has a reputation of the world's finest food.

However, old ways of preparing these original and authentic recipes are slowly dying. Ceramic clays, wooden spoons, and open fire are the thing of the past, and we are slowly drawn into the modern ways of life which demand fast cooking methods. We simply don't have an entire day to waste with a pot of beef stew or slow-cooked beans, but we still want a good, tasty, and nourishing dinner. And this is where your slow cooker comes in. It is a perfect appliance designed to make your life simple and your dinner healthy and tasty.

I have to admit that I was a bit skeptical when buying my first slow cooker. It sounded too good to be true. So many cooking advantages, extremely easy to use, no need for additional pans and skillets, or special supervision while cooking, and forgetting about the mess in the kitchen! Just like every other appliance, you have to spend some time with your slow cooker in order to learn how to cook with it. The biggest advantage, in my opinion, is the name – slow cooking. I was thrilled with the idea that one single appliance will give me those old-fashioned grandmother's recipes, that I craved for so much! But forget about the rest. Just like our grandmothers made a mess in the kitchen, you will have to get your hands a bit dirty too. Some meals do require additional skillets and pans, especially if you're after the authentic Mediterranean recipes and some desserts. For a superb taste and the food that will achieve the state of art, you will have to supervise it. Each meat part is different, each vegetable requires different liquid amounts, even two different rice types will not react the same in the cooker. This is inevitable, but the single bite of slowly cooked food will make you forget about it. That, I promise.

The second enormous advantage of your slow cooker is the nutritional value of the food. Slow cooking reduces the destruction and the loss of important nutrients, especially vitamins. Not only that your food will be healthier, but this also means a better taste. And if you're a fanatic like me, you will always choose fresh ingredients instead of frozen. These are healthier, tastier, and easier to handle in your slow cooker.

The biggest secret of slow cooking is time. This seems to confuse most of the people who are trying to prepare their meals in this rather simple kitchen appliance. I guess it's like with everything else – with time you will get that chef's 'feeling' for cooking. But for the beginning, simply adjust the entire process to your schedule. Just like in every other pan, the lower the temperature, the longer it takes to cook. The same basic principle goes for ingredients. Tender and smaller meat parts, for example, need less cooking, and vice versa. I do understand that this can be a bit tricky and that's why I have used the easiest and the most convenient setting – **low**. You can easily prepare the ingredients the day before, throw them in your slow cooker, and set the heat to low. The cooker will need all day to prepare the food, but it will also mean that most of the ingredients will be properly cooked and you will have a nice dinner at the end of a day.

Most people will say that a slow cooker is all about throwing the ingredients in the cooker and simply closing the lid, there are some things to keep in mind if you want your meal to come out right. For the best results, experts recommend that the vessel should be *half to two-thirds full*. For soups and other dishes that need to simmer, leave about **4-inches** between food and the top of the vessel. Ingredients that need *longer* cooking such as meat and root vegetables should be at the **bottom** of a slow cooker so that they have a maximum exposure to the heat source.

More delicate ingredients like rice, pasta, certain vegetables and dairy products should be added during the *last hour* of cooking. These simple tricks will give you the best possible results in your slow cooker.

Another important detail to keep in mind when using your slow cooker is the lid. It is necessary to keep the lid sealed to avoid any heat loss. Otherwise, it will slow down the cooking process and change the entire meal. However, this rule doesn't apply when there is some occasional stirring. This depends on the recipe you're preparing.

When it comes to seasoning and spices, throwing them in a cooker with other ingredients is perfectly fine. However, if you have some time to spend with your slow cooker, you might consider taking the most out of them as well. The flavor of different spices will be best preserved if they're added at the *end* of the cooking process. This means that you should wait until the meal is fully cooked and then gently stir in the spices. The same goes for herbs. Adding the herbs *after* the cooking is completed will prevent them to change color and lose flavor.

The slow cooker is not a science. In no time you will be able to turn every recipe into a slow-cooked meal. You just need some time and practice. And the best part about it – you're not limited to the certain recipes. The slow cooker is not reserved for stews and beans. Soon enough you will find out that almost every recipe can be prepared in this amazing kitchen appliance. Enjoy it!

First, you have to know that there are several different types of slow cookers. The most common ones are ceramic and porcelain. If you're looking for a high-quality cooker and you're willing to pay a little more money, then I would suggest that you choose ceramic slow cooker. In my experience, these slow-cookers have the best temperature distribution system and most of are removable which is perfect for cleaning. The third option would be a metal cooker. It's probably the cheapest type, but won't last long.

Regarding the size of your slow cooker, that really depends on how many people you're having for dinner. There are three standard categories of slow cookers:

1. **Small** slow cookers are perfect for 1-2 people *(one to three-quart model)*.
2. **Medium** slow cookers will be enough to feed 3-4 people *(four to six-quart model)*.
3. **Large** slow cookers is the best option for 5-6 people *(eight-quart model)*.

Having a large family and not being able to cook all the time, I personally chose a large slow cooker. For me, it works the best being able to cook for a couple of days in advance and simply eat the leftovers. This is why all of my recipes are adjusted to this size. And if that's not your case, it's not a big deal. Reduce the ingredient quantities and simply prepare smaller quantities of food.

The next dilemma you will probably stumble upon would be a round or oval slow cooker. Round slow cookers are a good option if you're only planning to cook stews and soups in it. However, being a food fanatic myself, my plan was to try every possible meal in my new slow cooker. Round shapes weren't really getting along with my plans so I got myself an oval-shaped slow cooker. It was a good option because it works great for all types of food you can possibly imagine. But, there is one thing you should keep in mind, whatever shape you choose – the lid material. I have to admit that an opaque model does look better. However, they are not very practical. The slow cooker has one important trick – the lid should be kept on while cooking, as much as possible. Opening the lid all the time will let out the heat and extend the cooking time, and you probably don't want to add a couple of more hours to an already long cooking process. Therefore, you will be better off with a glass lid. This way, you will be able to see what's going on in your slow cooker all the time without having to open it.

Slow Cooker Features

Fancy buttons, timers, lights, and tons of options, unfortunately also mean more money. However, these are not just a decoration to your new kitchen appliance, and I like to say that I'm not rich enough to buy cheap stuff. These fancy buttons will make your cooking way easier and prevent the waste of good food. Surely, even the cheapest options have some basic settings of heat and timers, but you will definitely have to be a professional to handle one of those. If you're getting a slow cooker for the first time in your life, make sure to invest some more in order to make the machine work for you as much as possible. What I like the most about more expensive models are the different programs for different kinds of food. This can be quite handy if you're not really sure about the main ingredient in your meal. Other important features of high-quality models include: indicator lights and sounds, timers, and auto-cooking option.

Indicator lights and sounds are especially important for slow cookers. This simple feature will let you know whether the cooker is working or not. Slow cookers take a while to heat up and without this feature you won't be able to know if your cooker is working or not. And if you're like me and just want to throw the ingredients in your cooker and go to work without having to wait, this option is extremely useful.

Timers are probably the best feature a slow cooker has to offer, and not all models have them. Honestly, most of the time you'll be away while the cooker works (we are talking about 6-8 or even more hours). So once the cooking time has been reached, your cooker will simply switch to another perfect timer setting – 'keep warm' option. This means that your cooker will be constantly heating up your food, over a minimum temperature, and you'll get a nice warm meal when you get back home from work.

And the last, but not the least option is auto-cooking. Only the best slow cookers have it. In this case, your cooker will start the cooking process on high, as it should be, and then reduce the heat to low. This method is proven to be the best for all cooking methods, not just slow-cooking.

Another important tip I have to mention is the space. Before buying a slow cooker, make sure you have enough space for it. Most manufacturers advise that a slow cooker should be at least 6 inches away from any other appliances in the kitchen. Although a good slow cooker never gets too hot to cause some serious damage, you should keep in mind that it will work for a long time and your other appliances will be exposed to some mild heat for hours. This is not the best scenario, which is probably why you should clear some space for it.

Preparing food for your slow cooker recipe. There are some basic guidelines when preparing the food for cooking that you won't find in the recipes. You should never chop or slice the vegetables hours before cooking. This means fewer vitamins and less taste, and more unnatural color. The best option would be to prepare your vegetables right before cooking. This, however, is not mandatory for meat. On the contrary, most of the recipes require some marinades, which is why you can prepare your meat cuts even the night before and allow it to rest in some nice marinade in the refrigerator. And if you have some time to spare, the best culinary trick is to brown your meat before the actual cooking. This will give you that nice crispy flavor everybody loves.

Making layers in your slow cooker depends on the recipe, but some basic rules are simple and understandable. The first layer is directly exposed to heat, which means it will soften the most. If your recipe doesn't mention different, always choose some thick meat cuts for the basis of your recipe and leave the tender vegetables on top.

Adjust the seasonings according to the recipe. If your meal is prepared in layers, then make sure to sprinkle some salt and pepper on each layer. This rule doesn't apply for most herbs. If you have some extra time and you will be next to your cooker while cooking, make sure to add herbs right before the cooking ends.

This will save flavors and colors of your herbs and prevent them from being totally destroyed in the cooking process.

For the end, add the required liquid in your recipe and close the lid tightly. It is very important that the lid fits perfectly or it won't cook your food effectively. Make sure to check this before even buying your slow cooker.

After you have prepared everything, you should choose the heat settings. I personally love **low** settings, which cook for eight to ten or even twelve hours. This way you will get a perfectly tender meat and vegetables you simply can't have on high settings, which usually cook for four to six hours.

As I said before, make sure you keep the lid on as much as possible for the recipe. Every time you remove the lid you will extend the precious time of cooking. Another important tip is to avoid stirring the food while cooking. The slow cooker has an amazing heat distribution system, so any additional stirring is really not necessary – it just requires removing the lid all the time.

Now, all you have to do is letting it cook. This is the best part about the slow cooker – enjoy your day without having to be there all the time. When you hear the indicator sound telling you that the cooking is finished, simply serve your meal and enjoy!

CHAPTER TWO

All About Mediterranean Cheese

Traditional ways of making cheese in the Mediterranean region have been cherished for centuries as a symbol and a true trademark of the Mediterranean cuisine. Even today, it is almost impossible to imagine a day without a good slice of cheese usually sprinkled with some olive oil and served with a meal. And no wonder why! The authentic Mediterranean cheese types are worldwide recognized delicacies. From France and Italy to Greece and Turkey – all Mediterranean regions have kept their traditional methods of producing the best possible cheese on the market which makes this region a leading expert in this industry.

There are hundreds of cheese types all over the Mediterranean region and they are usually made from cow's, goat's, sheep or buffalo milk with one thing in common – a unique diversity of cheese making processes and distinctive flavors. Every single cheese type is followed by hundreds of different recipes which contribute to the enormous health benefits and popularity of this diet. Cheese contains significant amounts of vitamins A and D. It is a good source of proteins and several types of minerals. Its calcium content is simply amazing. Just one ounce of mozzarella cheese, for example, will give you about 200 milligrams of calcium! It is a fifth of your recommended dietary needs which is simply mind-blowing!

Even though the Mediterranean superstar, Greek yogurt, has the highest amounts of proteins found in dairy products (about 18 grams), every other hard cheese will provide about 8 grams of proteins. This is really fascinating if you consider that an average man needs about 56 grams of proteins per day and the average woman about 46. In translation, one traditional Mediterranean breakfast will give you plenty of proteins in a small amount of food.

Most cheese types are extremely rich in vitamin B12, vitamin A, vitamin K2, zinc, selenium, phosphorous, sodium, and riboflavin. This, of course, goes for organic, unprocessed, and naturally produced cheese types that are almost impossible to find outside the Mediterranean region.

Cheese is also famous for their probiotics – good bacteria that help regulate the intestinal microflora. Maintaining a healthy gut environment is crucial for a good health. It prevents so many different health problems, from digestive tract and brain to heart health. Healthy gut flora is especially important after different antibiotics we all have to take from time to time. Eating lots of dairy products will help restore the balance between good and bad bacteria and strengthen your entire organism.

These are just some of the "side effects" of this super-healthy lifestyle. Eating cheese in the Mediterranean region is part of a tradition. You eat it because you love it, as simple as that! But with every single bite of perfectly soft goat's cheese sprinkled with extra virgin olive oil and served with fresh olives and herbs, your organism will enjoy the benefits it has to offer. These are some of the most famous traditional cheese types served daily in every house in the entire Mediterranean region:

Feta

The famous feta cheese comes from Greece. Its long tradition goes way back to Homer who mentioned the preparation of this cheese in his famous book 'Odyssey'. Feta gained its popularity all over Europe and it's produced in many countries like Germany, France, and Denmark, but the name and the recipe are protected. Creamy and soft feta is made from sheep's milk, or a mixture of goat's and sheep's milk. Today, you can find some types of feta made from cow's milk, but it's not authentic nor a high-quality cheese.

The superb taste of this cheese justifies its glory in so many different recipes. It is a true delicacy when combined with olive oil and different Mediterranean herbs and spices. It is unique and irreplaceable in fresh vegetable salad recipes where it gives a nice, salty balance and creamy texture. It is very difficult to replace a high-quality feta cheese, but if you have to do it, the best substitutes would ricotta, Halloumi (Greek sort of cheese), Mexican Queso-Fresco cheese, and tofu as a vegan option.

Parmesan

Italy has a long tradition of making cheese. This Mediterranean region has a great geographical position and a perfect climate for animal breeding. Different dairy products are irreplaceable and a tradition of good cheese production goes way back to the middle ages. Parmesan cheese is named after the town Parma and Reggio Emilia in North Italy. The original recipe was jealously kept in every family for generations which made Parmesan cheese a true culinary delicacy. The basic recipe includes skimmed cow's milk, hard texture, and rich, fruity taste.

Italy offers lots of high-quality cheese types. However, the most famous ones are Parmesan, Mozzarella, Ricotta, and Mascarpone. Parmesan is definitely "the king of Italian cheese" with the two most important types - Parmigiano-Reggiano and Grana Padano. Both types are equally good and tasty and the only difference is the production method.

Grana Padano comes from the region of Lombardy, Northern Italy. This cheese is characteristic for its rich flavor and ideal texture for shredding. There are many substitutes for Parmesan cheese like Asiago, Romano, and Spanish Manchego Viejo.

Mozzarella

Another Italian national specialty and a true delicacy of the entire Mediterranean is Mozzarella Cheese. Mozzarella is mostly used for pizzas and salads, but its neutral taste makes it perfect even for cakes. It silky soft texture, tender and delicate taste shouldn't fool you. Even though it's very hard to resist its perfect taste, mozzarella is a full-fat cheese and you should keep that in mind.

Probably the most famous Mediterranean mozzarella combination is with fresh juicy tomatoes, olive oil, and fresh basil. Without any doubt, this is one of the healthiest snacks you can serve during the hot summer days. But if you don't have a nice piece of mozzarella at hand, there are some reasonably good substitutes – Queso Oaxaco, Bel Paese, Provolone Cheese, or Caciocavallo.

Manchego

For hundreds of years, this cheese was produced in south-central Spain, in the region of La Mancha. The milk used in making the manchego cheese comes from the Manchega sheep, an ancient breed adapted to the dry flat region of La Mancha. The long tradition of keeping the cheese deep in the caves during the maturation process is still widely spread in that region which is exactly what makes manchego a true heritage of the Mediterranean. Its hard and nutty flavor is rarely found outside the Spain which makes this cheese extremely difficult to replace in the recipes.

„Sack Cheese"

There are no written documents about the origins of this cheese. However, for the past couple of centuries, this cheese was a natural treasure of Balkan countries like Croatia, Bosnia and Herzegovina, Serbia, and Montenegro. The original recipe included cow's milk, but there are plenty of variations with goat's milk.

A technique of making this cheese was discovered by accident when people tried to find the best way to preserve their milk during winter months. Today, this type of cheese is probably the only Mediterranean cheese that is not industrialized and can only be found in small family farms who cherish the recipe and the culture of its production. If you ever get your hands on this cheese, I recommend a combination with baked potatoes, dried meat, olives, and wine.

Caciocavallo

Caciocavallo comes from the southern regions of Italy. This semi-soft, cow's cheese has a light-yellow color with a couple of very small holes in it. It is produced in a bell or gourd-shaped form. Traditionally, two of the gourds are tied together by the neck and hung over a horizontal pole to dry. This practice is still used in some areas. Caciocavallo is perfect for pizzas and casseroles, sandwiches, salads, and pies.

Van Herbed Cheese

(Turkish: 'Van Otlu Peyniri')

Van herbed cheese is a type of cheese made from sheep's or cow's milk. It is characteristic for different herbs that are added to the ripened cheese. This beautiful Turkish cheese has about 200 years old tradition and it is famous for its semi-hard texture and salty taste with a perfect aroma of garlic, thyme, and other 25 different herbs that are contained in the original recipe. The most popular type of Van herbed cheese is definitely Otlu cheese produced in the Van Province of Turkey.

A wonderful mixture of different herbs and spices makes this cheese impossible to replace with any other cheese in the world.

Provolone Cheese

Another Italian delicacy whose texture and taste is very similar to mozzarella. Just like mozzarella, provolone is semi-soft, cow's milk cheese. The production method includes stretching the curds and forming the cheese which is then cured for two to three months.

Provolone is famous as a perfect addition to sandwiches, snacks, and desserts. It can replace mozzarella in every single recipe.

CHAPTER THREE

Mediterranean Herbs and Spices

Their homeland is where the sea meets the sun and the stone. Rosemary, parsley, basil, dill, thyme, sage, fennel, oregano, laurel and many other bring the irresistible Mediterranean scents and flavors directly in our kitchen no matter where we live.

Tasty and nutritious, fresh and dried, Mediterranean herbs and spices not only please the taste but the health as well. They play an important role in our diet while giving a special tone and impression of certain dishes. Despite their low-calorie values, herbs definitely have amazing healing properties and they are widely used in medicine and cosmetic industry. These properties were recognized even in ancient times. Some great civilizations like Greece, Egypt, and China used herbs and spices as a part of their cultural rituals and popular medicine. Trading with these valuable items, especially different oils, was highly respected and well paid.

Today, there are lots of different scientific studies that confirm these traditional assumptions. Different herbs that are the main component of the entire Mediterranean diet are an enormous source of different nutrients and can help prevent different health issues. The typical and most common Mediterranean herbs and spices are garlic, basil, parsley, dill, thyme, rosemary, sage, bay leaves, cayenne pepper,

paprika, oregano, and saffron. Without any doubt, the Mediterranean cuisine takes advantage of these healthy culinary plants in every single dish which make it the healthiest diet in the world. Now let's go through the most common Mediterranean spices...

Garlic

"Let food be thy medicine, and medicine be thy food." Those are famous words from the ancient Greek physician Hippocrates, often called the father of Western medicine. He actually used to prescribe garlic to treat a variety of medical conditions, and no wonder why!

It is believed that this member of the lily family came all the way from the Central Asia to the Mediterranean area, where it found its new home and became an important part of the recognizable taste of the Mediterranean cuisine.

There are over 200 active substances in this incredible plant that are healthy for the entire body. In a traditional medicine, garlic plays one of the most important roles. Throughout history, during different epidemics of cholera, plague, dysentery, and other diseases, garlic was recommended as a primary cure and prevention. Even today, there are so many pills and medicines that are nothing else but garlic packed in capsules. Garlic is proven to have antiseptic, antibacterial and antifungal activity, and it is comparable to the best antibiotics. It is extremely rich in calcium, copper, potassium, phosphorus, iron, and vitamin B1. Besides, just 1 oz of garlic contains:

Manganese: 23% of the RDA.
Vitamin B6: 17% of the RDA.
Vitamin C: 15% of the RDA.
Selenium: 6% of the RDA.
Fiber: 1 gram.

Garlic is an aromatic spice without which most of the Mediterranean meals would be incomplete. It is one of the most used spices in the world. Fresh, dried, whole or ground, this remarkable spice surely has a lot to offer.

Along with many other nutrients, you can easily say that garlic contains a little bit of everything our body would possibly need.

Basil

Basil is one of the most popular spices in the Mediterranean cuisine. The name comes from the Greek language and it means „the royal herb". Its characteristic smell and taste are usually used with tomatoes or pestos for the final pinch in preparing stews, sauces, salads, marinades, and dressings. Basil goes perfectly and it is often combined with herbs like rosemary, oregano, parsley, and thyme.

A traditional medicine uses its healing properties for treating kidney diseases, depression, appetite problems, and menstrual cramps. Its anti-inflammatory properties are perfect for treating bronchitis, sore throat, and coughing.

Rosemary

Without any doubt, this is the most popular Mediterranean spice with many undeniable health benefits. The power of rosemary, especially its essential oil, is known since the ancient times and it's extensively used in a traditional medicine. Its healing abilities will help prevent and cure many different skin conditions, hair problems, digestive issues, migraines, and boost mental activities.

Italian cuisine is famous for rosemary. Fresh and finely chopped rosemary is added to different fish, veal, beef, and chicken recipes. Crushed rosemary is unreplaceable in stews, dressings, marinades, and the most famous of all — focaccia.

Parsley

Surely one of the most popular and used spice in the world of gastronomy, but especially in the Mediterranean cuisine. According to some sources, a homeland of parsley is Sardinia, an island in the Mediterranean Sea. This amazing leafy plant is a real treasury of different beneficial substances and an excellent source of vitamin C and B, minerals, and iron. A handful of parsley used mostly for garnishing will boost up an entire digestion tract and help your organism take the most out of your meal. These are just some of the reasons why parsley should become your 'must have' ingredient in the kitchen.

Dill

This aromatic, annual herb of the parsley family has fine blue-green leaves and yellow flowers. Today, Southern Europe is a natural home of dill, but it's believed that it comes from the ancient Persia and India. Its healing properties were first recognized by Arabs and Romans who used dill to treat stress, insomnia, and different types of poisoning. In the Balkan region, women used to wear dill in their shoes before the wedding believing it would help make their husbands faithful and loyal. But regardless of its history, one thing is certain – dill is a perfect addition to different sauces, soups, fish meals, and vegetarian dishes, and should definitely become highly appreciated ally in the kitchen.

Cayenne Pepper

The taste of a good stew, paprikash, goulash, slow-cooked meat and vegetables, rice, sauce, or even a cheese dish would definitely be incomplete without this super-spice. Its fine flavor, silky texture, and a passionate red color are a secret weapon of most culinary experts in the world. The main ingredient of cayenne peppers is capsaicin which is responsible for the recognizable spicy taste. It stimulates the parts of the brain responsible for the regulation of body temperature. This is why cayenne pepper is one of the best spices to use in the summer when the body needs an extra help to lower and regulate its temperature. Besides, cayenne pepper contains massive amounts of carotenoids, vitamin C, and flavonoids.

Bay Laurel - (Bay leaves)

For thousands of years, bay leaves have been a symbol of bravery and glory. This famous spice came to the Mediterranean region from Asia and became a symbol of the Mediterranean cuisine. It was often called the sacred god's wood or the Apollo's wood and played an important role in the Apollo's Temple at Delphi. Since it has some mildly narcotic substances, it would help the priests of the temple to induce the trance state. For centuries, bay leaves were believed to protect against lightning, diseases, and evil spirits. Although it won't do much good against the lightning, some studies prove that bay leaves are a great treatment of the respiratory system, skin problems, and rheumatic disorders. Besides, it contains some enzymes that help the protein breakdown which makes it a perfect addition to meat recipes.

Sage

It comes from the Latin word „salvare" which means „to be saved". Franciscan monasteries had been growing sage for decades. People believed in its healing powers so much that there was a saying that even death can't be cured with sage. These exaggerated attributes are the result of its natural antiseptic, antibiotic, and antioxidant components with a huge list of healing properties. Sage is used in treating a sore throat, flu, different wounds, respiratory problems, and as a beauty product. The best culinary use of the unique taste of sage is in heavy meals because it improves more difficult digestion of these foods.

Fennel

Fennel is a typical Mediterranean spice grown mostly in Greece, Turkey, Italy, Southern France, and North African countries. Fennel goes way back in history. Ancient Romans used it to add some extra flavors to their salads and even bread. In the middle ages, fennel spread around the Europe and the rest of the world, and it became one of the most popular plants in medicine. It was used and still is, to heal digestion problems, breathing problems, and to stimulate the appetite. Its healing effectiveness became so popular that people believed it could protect them against witchcraft and black magic.

Fennel is one of the most important spices in the Mediterranean cuisine and definitely the best one for your slow cooker. Besides stews, meat, and slow cooked vegetables, fennel will work perfectly with different fruit and vegetable combinations.

Oregano

Oregano is named by two Greek words, „oros" which means mountain, and „ganos" which means joy and happiness. Its impressive health benefits were recognized long time ago, by Hippocrates and Paracelsus. Both of them recommended oregano as a natural antioxidant and a medicine for various health issues like colds, headaches, digestive problems, stress, etc. This popular and the worldwide known spice came from the southern parts of Europe – Italy and Greece. It very common ingredient in Italian cuisine and irreplaceable part of every good pizza recipe.

Thyme

Thyme has been known for centuries as "a cure for the poor", and with a good reason. It was believed that its healing properties were so powerful that people used to bring it to temples to please the gods. Ancient Greeks and Egyptians used medical properties of thyme for thousands of years, but the true glory of thyme came in the middle ages in the times of plague. Its aromatic fragrance and antibiotic properties are extremely appreciated even today. Thyme stimulates all body functions, circulation, digestion, and boosts up the immune system. It is very effective in wound healing, in the treatment of the urinary tract and respiratory problems. The biggest natural habitat of thyme is Southern and Eastern Europe, and North Africa. It is a true culinary gem of the Mediterranean cuisine. It's used to spice up different meat, mushroom, and vegetable dishes. Dried thyme has much stronger taste than the fresh one, so it is important to have the right amount to transform your meal into a fairytale of flavors.

Saffron

The king of spices - saffron. It is the most expensive spice in the world. The high cost of saffron is reasonable because it takes around 1000 square meters to grow 150,000 flowers, and for just one kilogram of this amazing spice you need between 80,000 and 150,000 flowers. The bigger producers of saffron are Iran, France, Spain, Morocco, Turkey, and Austria and its total annual production is around 200 tons. However, the king of spices justifies its price with an incredibly sophisticated taste that will definitely turn your meal into a real poetry.

Authentic Mediterranean recipes use mostly fresh spices. However, this is not the case today and although freshly picked herbs are the best option, most of us don't have the opportunity to buy them throughout the year. This is why dried herbs and spices play an important role in a modern cooking. They can easily be bought in every store which is a great advantage if you're going after the authentic and original taste; and if used correctly, you can get the same effect like with fresh herbs and spices. The trick is to use half or the third of the amount given in the recipe because dried plants tend to have more intense flavor and smell. Once you master them, you will agree that spices are the best culinary companions. Use them humbly, knowingly, but also be playful and creative with them. Enjoy the smells of the Mediterranean nature and turn the simplest meal into a festival of flavors!

Celery

Celery has a very long tradition in the Mediterranean culture and cuisine. In ancient Roman Empire, this herb was a symbol of death and sadness, but later on, in history, it became a symbol of good luck and happiness with such an amazing culinary use of the entire plant. It plays an important role in every weight loss diet due to its low calorie and high dietary fiber content. It's a perfect addition to soups and salad and an inevitable part of the Mediterranean cuisine.

Nutmeg

This aromatic spice with its unique flavor came from South East Asia and found its place in all cuisines in the world. Its recognizable rich flavor comes from the essential oils which are the main ingredient of this amazing spice. Fresh nutmeg will give the best taste to your meal and can be added before the cooking. Dried nutmeg, on the other hand, is best as a final pinch at the end of cooking to give your meal a special note. It will work perfectly in different soup recipes, sauces, pies, sweets, and cakes.

Cinnamon

Cinnamon is known as one of the oldest spices in the world. First written history of cinnamon comes from ancient China, 2700 years ago, where it has been used as a medicine. In the middle ages, cinnamon was brought to Europe and found an extremely fertile ground in the Mediterranean region.

Today, it's impossible to imagine a dessert without a pinch of cinnamon. It's often added to cakes, fruit salads, cocoa, compotes, mulled wine, pies, etc.

Ginger

Ginger is famous for its culinary, medical, and aromatic properties. About 2,000 years ago Romans brought this spice to the Mediterranean, where it remained as a part of a local cuisine until Middle ages when the ginger spread all around Europe.

Health benefits of ginger are well known and confirmed in many studies. It has an amazing anti-inflammatory influence and the ability to boost up the entire immune system. Ginger can easily be combined with many different meals which is probably its biggest culinary advantage. It will perfectly spice up meat and poultry, but also every possible fruit and vegetable combination.

Cloves

Cloves are an Asian spice used for over 2,000 years in the islands of Indonesia. These aromatic flower buds were highly appreciated in ancient China and mentioned in their chronicles as one of the best breath refreshing tools. Cloves were brought to Europe and the Mediterranean region in the 4th century by Arab traders.

Cloves are very rich in eugenol, an active component that has been subject to many scientific studies about the digestive system and inflammation. This substance is excessively used in dentistry for root canal therapies. A culinary use of cloves is absolutely fabulous – from traditional pumpkin pies, mulled wine, to different holiday desserts. Cloves will also give a nice touch to soups, stews, and chilies.

Turmeric

Turmeric, or sometimes called curcuma, comes from the ginger family. This colorful spice comes from Eastern India where it has been used for thousands of years. Today, with its other cousins from the ginger family, it is one of the most popular spices in the world with 800,000 tons produced in a year. Turmeric has amazing healing abilities especially in treating digestive problems, infections, inflammation, and even cancer. In recipes, it will serve as a nice touch to stews, salads, soups, marinades, and dressings.

Soups

Brussel Sprouts Soup

 **5 Minutes**

 **8 Hours**

 **3 Servings**

About Brussel Sprouts Soup

Brussel sprouts are considered to be one of the healthiest foods in the world and there is a good reason for that. They are loaded with different vitamins and minerals. Being very low in saturated fats and cholesterol, Brussel sprouts are a perfect option for maintaining your body weight and optimum health. But this soup does little more than that. A creamy combination of these healthy ingredients and fresh mint for some extra taste will soon become one of your favorite soup options.

Nutritional Information

KCAL	PRT	CARB	FATS
194	10g	21.7g	9.8g

ww 6pts

Ingredients

1 lb fresh brussel sprouts, halved *0*
7 oz fresh baby spinach, torn *0*
1 tsp of sea salt *0*
1 cup of whole milk *7 pts*
3 tbsp of sour cream *4 pts*
1 tbsp of fresh celery, finely chopped *0*
1 tsp of granulated sugar *1 pt*
2 cups of water *0*
1 tbsp of butter *5 pts*

Preparation

1 Combine the ingredients in a slow cooker and securely close the lid. Set the heat to low and cook for 8 hours.

2 Open the cooker and transfer the soup to a food processor. Blend well to combine and serve.

Make It Different

I always like to play with different spices when preparing my meals. This recipe contains fresh mint for some extra taste, which I absolutely adore. Unfortunately, my family is not a big fan of the minty taste. For that reason, I was forced to try something different. To be honest, this soup is good as it is, without any special spices. However, I like the unique taste certain spices give to this soup. It's like having a different meal each time you prepare it, which works perfectly when you're not in a mood to think about your lunch. I found that one of the best spices for this soup is ginger. Replace the mint with just one teaspoon of freshly ground ginger and follow the recipe. Works perfect every time.

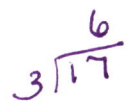

Classic Ragout Soup

 **5 Minutes**  **8 Hours**  **6 Servings**

About Classic Ragout Soup

Classic ragout soup is one of the best recipes to prepare in your slow cooker. This lamb based recipe with peas, carrot and potato is so filling and tasty that you will want to try all the possible combinations you can find. And that's the best part about this soup – everything is allowed. There are hundreds of different ragout recipes found in each part of the Mediterranean region and they all have one thing in common – a perfect taste of homemade, traditional cooking.

Nutritional Information

KCAL	PRT	CARB	FATS
307	24.9g	23.3g	13g

5 pts P/serve

Make It Different

If you have some spare time, try this simple trick to give your ragout an extra flavor. Heat up 2-3 tablespoons of olive oil in a large skillet. Add meat chops and briefly brown on both sides. Transfer to a slow cooker and follow the recipe. Frying the meat just before cooking doesn't take more than five minutes and will give you an extra crispy flavor you simply can't get by just cooking.

Ingredients

4 oz = 3 pts

1 lb lamb chops (1 inch thick)   1
1 cup of peas, rinsed   *4 pts*
4 medium-sized carrots, peeled and finely chopped   *0*
3 small onions, peeled and finely chopped   *0*
1 large potato, peeled and finely chopped   *2*   2
1 large tomato, peeled and roughly chopped   *0*
3 tbsp of extra virgin olive oil   *12 pts*
1 tbsp of cayenne pepper   *0*
1 tsp of salt   *0*
½ tsp of freshly ground black pepper   *0*

Preparation

Cut meat into bite-sized pieces. Make the first layer in your slow cooker. Now add peas, finely chopped carrots, onions, potatoes, and roughly chopped tomato.

Add about three tablespoons of olive oil, cayenne pepper, salt, and pepper. Give it a good stir and close the lid. Set for 8 hours on low.

Did You Know?

The word 'ragout' comes from France and it refers to a main stewed dish. The term itself comes from the word ragoûter which means 'to revive the taste'. The traditional method also includes slow-cooking over a minimum heat and that's exactly what makes this classic ragout one of the best recipes for your slow cooker.

You should never confuse classic ragout soup with Italian ragu. Unlike slow-cooked ragout based on different vegetables and meat, Italian ragu is a sauce used to dress pasta.

Gorgonzola Broccoli Soup

 **5 Minutes**

 **2 Hours**

 **4 Servings**

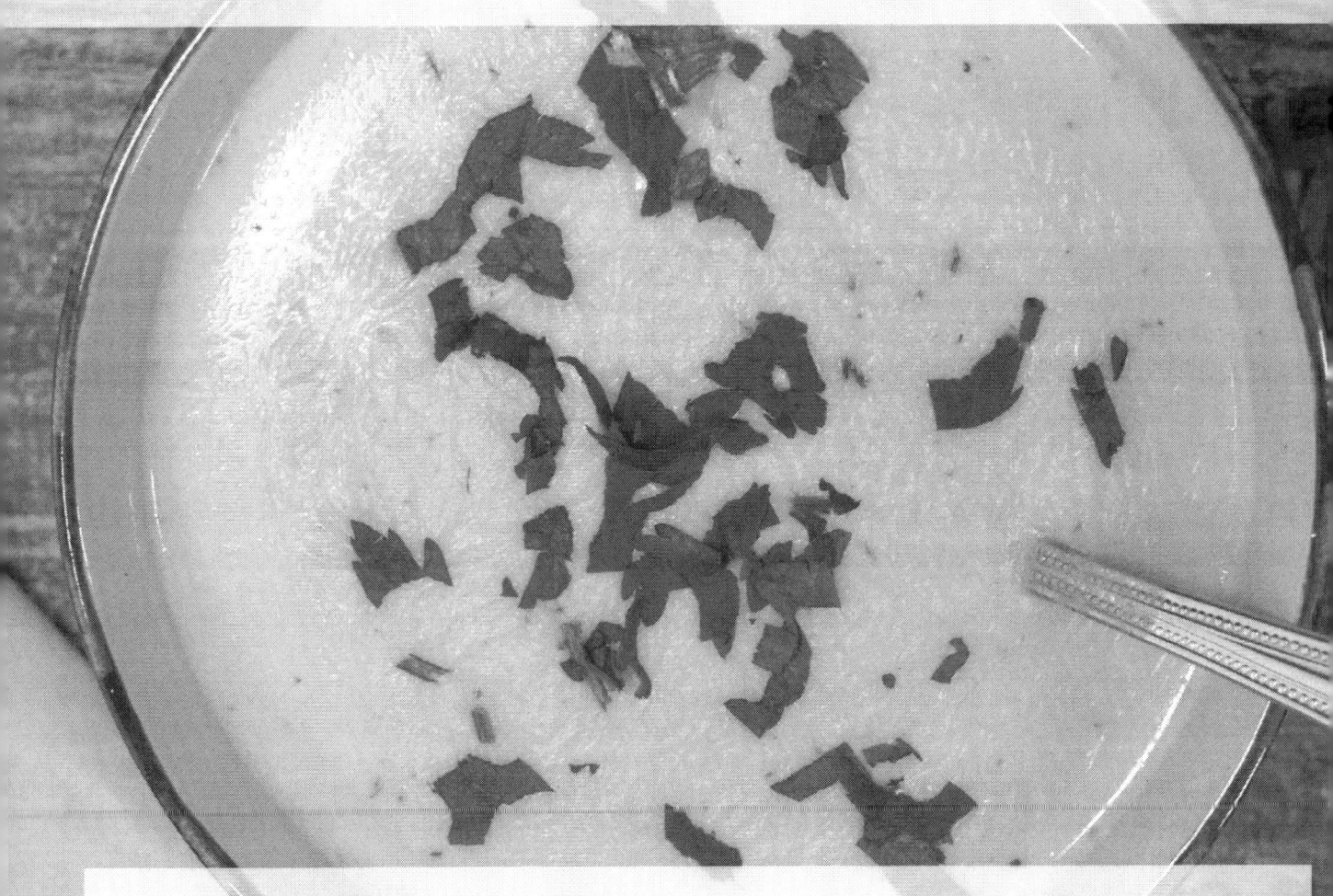

About Gorgonzola Broccoli Soup

Warm, creamy, and delicious! That's the best way to describe this bowl of the finest soup the Mediterranean region has to offer. Stir in some Greek yogurt or heavy cream right before serving and enjoy!

Nutritional Information

KCAL	PRT	CARB	FATS
208	11.8g	7.6g	15.8g

12 pts

Ingredients

10 oz of Gorgonzola cheese, crumbled *40*
1 cup of broccoli, finely chopped
1 tbsp of olive oil *4*
½ cup of full-fat milk *4*
½ cup of vegetable broth
1 tbsp of parsley, finely chopped
½ tsp of salt
¼ tsp of black pepper, ground

Preparation

1   Grease the bottom of a slow cooker with olive oil. Add all ingredients and three cups of water. Mix well with a kitchen whisker until fully combined.

2   Cover with a lid and cook for 2 hours on low settings.

3   Remove from the heat and sprinkle with some fresh parsley for extra taste.

4   I like to stir in one tablespoon of Greek yogurt before serving, but it's optional.

Did You Know?

Some research suggest that a tradition of making soups goes back as about 20,000 BC. Simple techniques as boiling water and cooking meat with vegetables were long used before the civilization introduced some new creative techniques.

The word soup itself comes from the French "soupe" (soup or broth). This is nothing but an old Latin term "suppa" used to describe a bread soaked in broth (a recipe probably picked up from old German tribes).

Today we know thousands of different soup recipes but still the most popular ones are different cream soups. People seem to enjoy the thick and creamy taste of broccoli, kale, mushrooms, cheese, cream, spices, etc. No wonder why...They really are something special. This particular recipe comes from France, from one of my many travels to the southern regions of this lovely country. I ordered a simple cream broccoli soup and received a true culinary delight. The secret was in melted gorgonzola combined with the finest olive oil. From that day forward, it became my favorite soup recipe and I wanted to share it with you. I hope you will enjoy it as much as I do!

Mercimek

 **5 Minutes**    **4-6 Hours**    **4 Servings**

About Mercimek

This famous Turkish red lentil soup is served in almost every restaurant. Its creamy texture and sweet taste of carrots combined with cumin make this soup one of my personal favorites. Serve with a few drops of lemon juice and enjoy!

Nutritional Information

KCAL	PRT	CARB	FATS
254	13.3g	34g	7.6g

Ingredients

1 cup of red lentils, soaked
1 medium-sized onion, peeled and finely chopped
½ cup of sweet carrot puree
1 tbsp of all-purpose flour
½ tsp of freshly ground black pepper
½ tsp of cumin, ground
½ tsp of salt
2 tbsp of olive oil

Preparation

1   Grease the slow cooker with olive oil and set the heat to high. Add finely chopped onion and one tablespoon of flour. Stir-fry for about ten minutes, stirring constantly.

2   Now add other ingredients and 4 cups of water. Close the lid and set the heat to low. Cook for 4-6 hours.

Did You Know?

Lentils are healthy, fulfilling, and delicious. They are an excellent source of protein, dietary fiber, iron, and potassium and were highly respected even in the ancient Greece. Hippocrates used to prescribe lentils for patients with liver ailments. Lentils definitely fall into the category of the oldest foods known to mankind, and the lentil soup was even mentioned in the Bible In Genesis 25:30-34, Esau is prepared to give up his birthright for a pot of fragrant red lentil soup (a "mess of pottage" in some versions) being cooked by his brother, Jacob. In Jewish tradition, lentil soup has been served at times of mourning, the roundness of the lentil representative of a complete cycle of life, while the eastern Muslim civilizations used lentils as one of the highly respected foods for different holidays.

I totally agree with tradition – lentils are special and definitely worth taking the time in the kitchen and preparing some amazing meals!

Moroccan Chickpea Soup

 **15 Minutes**  **7 Hours**  **6 Servings**

About Moroccan Chickpea Soup

This soup is not only the amazing change in your everyday eating habits, but it's also perfectly suitable for vegetarians and vegans. Chickpeas are an incredible source of proteins and dietary fibers. With almost neutral taste, they can easily be combined with different vegetables and spices. This tomato-tasting Moroccan soup with sweet carrot is both – refreshing and healthy. Sprinkle with some fresh parsley or a few drops of freshly squeezed lemon juice and enjoy!

Nutritional Information

KCAL	PRT	CARB	FATS
420	18.9g	58.6g	14g

Ingredients

14 oz chickpeas, soaked
2 large carrots, finely chopped
2 small onions, peeled and finely chopped
2 large tomatoes, peeled and finely chopped
3 tbsp of tomato paste
A handful of fresh parsley, finely chopped
2 cups of vegetable broth
3 tbsp of extra virgin olive oil
1 tsp of salt

Preparation

1   Soak the chickpeas overnight. Rinse and drain. Set side.

2   Grease the bottom of your slow cooker with three tablespoons of olive oil. Place the rinsed chickpeas, chopped onions, carrot, and finely chopped tomatoes.

3   Pour the vegetable broth and season with salt. Stir in tomato paste and securely lock the lid.

4   Set the heat to low and cook for 7 hours.

5   Sprinkle with fresh parsley and serve.

Did You Know?

Chickpeas are more than just a simple ingredient in your recipe. These amazing legumes help control blood sugar levels. The complex carbs found in chickpeas are slowly digested in our body and then used for energy. Chickpeas include starch. Unlike other carbs, this slow-burning carbohydrate doesn't lead to sudden spikes in energy levels which is great for weight control. Besides, proteins and fibers found in chickpeas help you feel full for hours, reduce food cravings and improve digestion. Fibers also help balance pH levels and bacteria found in your gut reducing so many different digestive problems. And that's not even all – chickpeas have been proven to help balance cholesterol levels and protect against heart disease. Having this said, it's time to give this amazing recipe a try.

Pumpkin Soup

 **5** Minutes    **4** Hours    **2** Servings

About Pumpkin Soup

Creamy pumpkin soup is among favorite soups in my household. Eating this picturesque yellow soup is always fun even for the youngest members of the family. This lovely soup is made with slowly stewed pureed pumpkin, ground turmeric for some nice flavor and color, and double cream for an extra creaminess. Serve immediately and have fun!

Nutritional Information

KCAL	PRT	CARB	FATS
215	5.6g	19.2g	14.3g

Ingredients

2 lb pumpkin, pureed
1 large onion, peeled and finely chopped
3 cups of vegetable broth
1 tbsp of ground turmeric
½ cup of double cream
½ tsp of salt
A handful of fresh parsley
3 tbsp of extra virgin olive oil

Preparation

1   Place finely chopped onion, pureed pumpkin, turmeric, salt, and olive oil in your slow cooker. Add vegetable broth and stir well.

2   Cover and set the heat to low. Cook for 4 hours. When done, remove the lid and stir in double cream. Top with some finely chopped parsley and serve.

Did You Know?

Pumpkin is a fast growing vine that belongs to a Cucurbitaceae family. It's one of the most popular field crops in the world. Its culinary use is absolutely amazing – from soups, stews, pies, to salads and desserts. But this orange plant is a little more than just a Halloween decoration. It is a true nutritive gold mine of different vitamins and minerals, and just a few calories. Its beta-carotene content is really admirable. This powerful antioxidant gives the plants its orange color and converts into a vitamin A once eaten. Beta-carotene is proven to reduce the risk of many different types of cancer; to prevent asthma, heart disease; and even delay a body degeneration. According to the Harvard School of Public Health's Department of Nutrition, high levels of beta-carotene found in pumpkin greatly reduce the risk of prostate cancer. Rich vitamin C, fiber, and potassium content in this amazing plant support long-term heart health and reduce hypertension. Increased potassium levels also reduce the risk of stroke, a decrease of bone density, kidney stones, and loss of muscle mass.

Pumpkin seeds, on the other hand, are extremely rich in manganese, phosphorus, copper, zinc, iron, and vitamin E. A great diversity of antioxidants found in these seeds make them an irreplaceable part of a healthy diet. Eat as a snack or toss a handful of pumpkin seeds into fruit/vegetable salad and take the most out of these little nutritive bombs.

Spring Spinach Soup

 **15-20 Minutes**

 **8 Hours**

 **5 Servings**

About Spring Spinach Soup

This old-fashioned, grandmother's recipe is truly amazing! A light lamb soup, full of proteins and other extremely important nutrients can easily replace dinner or even lunch. Spinach is an excellent source of vitamins A, C, E, and K, folates, sodium, potassium, calcium, copper, iron, magnesium, and manganese. When combined with lots of proteins from meat and eggs, you get something worth mentioning.

Nutritional Information

KCAL	PRT	CARB	FATS
325	34.6g	3.4g	19g

Ingredients

1 lb of lamb shoulder, cut into bite-sized pieces
12 oz fresh spinach leaves, torn
3 eggs, beaten
4 cups of vegetable broth
3 tbsp of extra virgin olive oil
1 tsp of salt

Preparation

1   Rinse and drain each spinach leaf. Cut into bite-sized pieces. Place in a slow cooker.

2   Sprinkle the meat generously with salt and transfer to a cooker. Add other ingredients and whisk in three beaten eggs. Close the lid and cook for 8 hours on low.

Did You Know?

Spinach is a true nutrition superstar. Its neutral taste and very few calories make it one of the best possible ingredients to prepare soups, stews, salad, smoothies, pies, etc. Although it has only 23 calories per 100 grams, spinach is one of the finest sources of dietary fibers and iron. These leafy greens are an excellent source of antioxidant vitamins like vitamin A and vitamin C; and other anti-oxidants like lutein, zea -xanthin and beta-carotene. All of this is extremely important in fighting off aging and various diseases. Besides, fresh spinach leaves provide 402% of daily vitamin-K requirements. This vitamin is vital for the bone building activity and preventing different neuronal damages in the brain. In addition to that, this healthy vegetable is a perfect source of many different B-complex vitamins like vitamin B6, thiamin, riboflavin, folates, and niacin. All of this makes spinach one of the best possible vegetables you can include in your daily diet.

The Sultan's Soup

 **10 Minutes**  **8 Hours**  **4 Servings**

About The Sultan's Soup

This heavy soup is based on beef, veal, or chicken broth and always combined with highly nutritive okra. In olden days, okra was rare, expensive, and considered as an aphrodisiac – only the richest people could afford it. That's probably how the soup got its name. True or not, even today this luxurious soup can proudly be served at some major holidays and family reunions.

Nutritional Information

KCAL	PRT	CARB	FATS
161	2.8g	9.1g	13g

Ingredients

3.5 oz of carrots, finely chopped
3.5 oz of celery root, finely chopped
A handful of green peas, soaked
A handful of fresh okra
2 tbsp of butter
2 tbsp of fresh parsley, finely chopped
1 egg yolk
2 tbsp of kaymak cheese
¼ cup of freshly squeezed lemon juice
1 bay leaf
1 tsp of salt
½ tsp of pepper
4 cups of beef broth plus one cup of water

Preparation

1   Preparing this lovely soup in a slow cooker is very easy. Combine the ingredients in a slow cooker and close the lid. Set the heat to low and cook for 8 hours.

2   Serve warm and enjoy!

Make It Different

If you really want to make this soup as authentic as possible, then you will need some more ingredients. The original recipe includes two different types of meat – veal and beef. Cut the tender parts of meat into bite-sized pieces and combine with other ingredients. For the recipe above, you will need about one pound of meat (combined) and one more cup of liquid, preferably beef broth. It does take some more time and effort to prepare the original recipe, but it's worth it. The cooking time will be 8-10 hours on low heat.

Tomato Soup

 **10 Minutes**  **5 Hours**  **5 Servings**

About Tomato Soup

This tomato soup has such a lovely color that makes me hungry every time I see it. I like to add some white beans or peas to boost up the nutritional values, but that is optional. Just make sure not to forget the creamy topping which goes perfectly with this soup.

Nutritional Information

KCAL	PRT	CARB	FATS
317	12.8g	34.9g	15.5g

Ingredients

2 lbs of medium-sized tomatoes, diced
1 cup of white beans, pre-cooked
1 small onion, diced
2 garlic cloves, crushed
1 cup of heavy cream
1 cup of vegetable broth
2 tbsp of fresh parsley, finely chopped
¼ tsp of black pepper, ground
2 tbsp of extra virgin olive oil
1 tsp of sugar
½ tsp of salt

Preparation

1   Grease the bottom of your cooker with olive oil. Set the heat to high and heat up. Add chopped onion and garlic. Briefly stir-fry, for 2 minutes. Now add tomatoes, white beans, vegetable broth, two cups of water, parsley, salt, pepper, and some sugar to balance the bitterness.

2   Reduce the heat to low and cook for 5 hours on low, or 3 hours on high.

3   Top with one tablespoon of sour cream and chopped parsley before serving.

Did You Know?

Tomatoes are famous for their lovely red color and bittersweet taste that everybody likes. This healthy vegetable is an irreplaceable part of so many different recipes, especially in the Mediterranean area where eating tomatoes is considered almost as a ritual. And I totally agree with that! Tomatoes are an excellent source vitamin C, biotin, molybdenum and vitamin K and should be included in your diet as much as possible. They are also a very good source of copper, potassium, manganese, dietary fiber, vitamin A (in the form of beta-carotene), vitamin B6, folate, niacin, vitamin E and phosphorus. In short – use them whenever you can and enjoy their valuable nutrients every day.

Vegetarian

Barbunya Pilaki

 **5** Minutes

 **8-10** Hours

 **6** Servings

About Barbunya Pilaki

Made with cranberry beans, this traditional Turkish recipe is filling, healthy, heart-warming, and perfect for your slow cooker. Combined with tomatoes, carrots, onions, and olive oil, barbunya pilaki can be served as a main dish, or a classic Turkish mezze. For this recipe, I have decided to prepare my beans in a slow cooker and to serve it with some boiled rice topped with grated Parmesan cheese. However, this meal is perfect as it is. Just pour it in a bowl after a long day and you're good to go.

Nutritional Information

KCAL	PRT	CARB	FATS
329	16.5g	50.9g	8g

Ingredients

2 cups of cranberry beans (I used fresh, but you can use dried beans instead)
2 medium-sized onions, peeled and finely chopped
3 large carrots, cleaned and chopped
3 large tomatoes, peeled and finely chopped
3 tbsp of extra virgin olive oil
2 tsp of granulated sugar
A handful of fresh parsley
2 cups of water

Preparation

1   Soak the beans overnight. Rinse and set aside.

2   Grease the bottom of your slow cooker with olive oil. Add other ingredients and pour two cups of water. Securely lock the lid and set the heat to low. Cook for 8-10 hours.

Did You Know?

The cranberry bean (also known as the borlotti bean) is widely used in Italian, Portuguese, Greek, and Turkish Cuisine. These lovely beans that look similar to the pinto beans, but larger with creamy white color, are originally from Colombia. Their smooth and neutral taste, easy preparation, and significant nutritive values gained popularity all over the world, especially in the Mediterranean region. The most famous of all recipes is definitely Turkish Barbunya Pilaki based on tomatoes and olive oil. Pilaki is a type of Turkish mezze (an appetizer) made with vegetables and beans that are cooked with onions, garlic, olive oil, and sugar.

Barbunya pilaki is a perfect idea to replace the usual appetizers for your friends and family. Sprinkle with a few drops of lemon juice right before serving, add some grated Parmesan cheese and enjoy this Mediterranean dish.

Braised Swiss Chard

 **15** Minutes  **6-8** Hours  **4** Servings

About Braised Swiss Chard

This recipe is one of the healthiest recipes in this cookbook. Tender Swiss chard with olive oil and potatoes is so simple yet tasty that you will fall in love it. It is usually served as a side dish accompanying grilled fish and meat. However, I like to serve it cold with a simple loaf of bread and a few drops of freshly squeezed lemon juice. The choice is yours!

Nutritional Information

KCAL	PRT	CARB	FATS
204	3.8g	21g	13g

Ingredients

1 lb of Swiss chard, torn (keep the stems)
2 medium-sized potatoes, peeled
and finely chopped
¼ cup of extra virgin olive oil
1 tsp of salt

Preparation

1 Place torn Swiss chard in a large, heavy-bottomed pot. Add enough water to cover and bring it to a boil. Briefly cook, for about two minutes until greens are tender. Drain in a colander and transfer to a slow cooker. Add finely chopped potatoes, olive oil, salt, and about one cup of water.

2 Cover and set the heat to low. Cook for 6-8 hours.

Did You Know?

Swiss chard is widely spread in the entire Mediterranean cuisine, mostly braised with other greens and olive oil and served with fish, meat, and poultry. It has been a part of traditional medicine for centuries when treating open wounds, ulcers, bladder inflammation, and kidneys.

This amazing vegetable is full of powerful antioxidants which prevent and fight free radical damage, inflammation, and disease development. On top of this, Swiss chard is an extremely rich source of potassium, magnesium, calcium, copper, and many minerals. With an impressive amount of vitamin K, vitamin A, and vitamin C, this vegetable is a true natural medicine for so many diseases and conditions.

Cold Cauliflower Salad

 **10 Minutes**  **6-8 Hours**  **4 Servings**

About Cold Cauliflower Salad

This lovely cold salad is so typical for the entire Mediterranean region. It is usually served as a light dinner option or a side dish. It goes perfectly with fish, meat, or as an appetizer. However you chose to serve it, one thing is certain – you will be getting some amazing nutrients. Cauliflower and broccoli are one of the healthiest vegetables you can possibly eat. When you combine that with garlic and extra virgin olive oil, you get one extremely nutritive meal for the entire family. Sprinkle with some dry rosemary for an extra taste and enjoy!

Nutritional Information

KCAL	PRT	CARB	FATS
182	5.7g	15.1g	13.2g

Ingredients

1 lb cauliflower florets
1 lb broccoli
4 garlic cloves, crushed
¼ cup of extra virgin olive oil
1 tsp of salt
1 tbsp of dry rosemary, crushed

Preparation

1 Rinse and drain the vegetables. Cut into bite-sized pieces and place in a slow cooker. Add olive oil and one cup of water. Season with salt, crushed garlic and dry rosemary.

2 Close the lid and set the heat to low. Cook for 6-8 hours.

3 Chill well before serving.

Did You Know?

More than 300 scientific research confirm that broccoli is the ultimate fighting champion against different types of cancer. Every single day we expose our body to different toxic substances, allergy-triggering substances, over the counter medicine, bad nutrition, and general poor lifestyle habits. This consequently leads to a major inflammation process in our body weakening our natural detoxification and immune system with a potential risk of cancer development. With its amazing nutritional values and detoxifying capabilities, broccoli helps clean and regenerate our entire organism. When combined with nutritionally similar cauliflower, powerful garlic, and omega-3 fatty acids rich olive oil, this salad is definitely a tasty proof that a food CAN be the best medicine.

Creamy Leblebi Stew

About Creamy Leblebi Stew

This creamy chickpea stew with the bittersweet taste of tomatoes and the smallest amount of cumin seeds is full of proteins and fibers that will fill you up in no time. It's perfect for vegetarians and can easily replace a full meal or serve as an appetizer. Sprinkle with some fresh parsley before serving and enjoy!

Nutritional Information

KCAL	PRT	CARB	FATS
340	13.2g	36.3g	17.1g

Ingredients

7 oz chickpeas, soaked overnight
1 large tomato, peeled and finely chopped
1 medium-sized red onion, peeled
and finely chopped
1 tbsp of cumin seeds
2 cups of vegetable broth
2 tbsp of extra virgin olive oil
2 tbsp of butter
1 tbsp of cayenne pepper
1 tsp of salt
2 tbsp of fresh parsley (for serving)

Preparation

1 Grease the bottom of a slow cooker with olive oil and place roughly chopped tomato and onion. Now add cumin seeds, chickpeas, and vegetable broth. Cover the lid and cook for 8 hours on low.

2 Remove the lid, and transfer to a food processor.

3 Stir in two tablespoons of butter and cayenne pepper. Season with salt and chopped parsley.

Did You Know?

Leblebi (a Turkish word for chickpea) is a very common ingredient in lots of different Mediterranean meals. This protein and fiber rich food is used in different soups, stews, vegetable spreads, desserts, and as a basis of a famous hummus. Their nutty flavor, buttery texture, and high nutrition values make them worth your time. And that is exactly why you should try another famous chickpea recipe – falafel. This recipe is quite simple. Mash chickpeas with garlic, cumin, coriander, and chili to taste. Divide the mixture into separate, bite-sized balls and briefly fry in olive oil. Serve with sour cream, yogurt, or tomato sauce.

Eggplant Moussaka

 **20-25 Minutes**  **4 Hours**  **4 Servings**

About Eggplant Moussaka

This fabulous recipe comes from Greece. They serve it cold with a drizzle of freshly squeezed lemon juice and just a couple of drops of olive oil which is a great idea because this meal can stand in the refrigerator for days. I prefer to serve it warm while the kaymak is still melting on top. Whatever you choose, make sure to use the top quality ingredients and get the best out of these lovely moussaka bites!

Nutritional Information

KCAL	PRT	CARB	FATS
250	11.7g	10.8g	19.2g

Ingredients

1 large eggplant, sliced
5 oz of mozzarella
3.5 oz kaymak cheese
2 medium-sized tomatoes, sliced
¼ cup of extra virgin olive oil
1 tsp of salt
½ tsp of freshly ground black pepper
1 tsp of oregano, dried

Preparation

1 Grease the bottom of your slow cooker with some olive oil. Slice the eggplant and make a layer in the cooker. Now add one slice of mozzarella and then one slice of tomato on each eggplant. Top with eggplant and kaymak. You can repeat the process until you have used all the ingredients.

2 Meanwhile combine olive oil with salt, pepper, and dried oregano. Pour the mixture over the moussaka, add about ½ cup of water and close the lid.

3 Set the heat to low and cook for 4 hours. You don't want to overcook it because it will lose its shape.

4 Serve immediately or even refrigerate overnight.

Did You Know?

Eggplants love layers in meals and most chefs agree that it's probably the best way to prepare them. In Italy, Turkey and Greece, eggplants are an irreplaceable part of famous baked dishes like eggplant alla parmigiana and moussaka. Grilled slices of eggplant go perfectly with tomato sauces, fresh basil, oregano, rosemary, slices of mozzarella, and parmesan cheese.

This recipe is just one variation of these traditional ways of preparing them. For some extra nutrition, you can add a layer of ground beef or top with creamy bechamel sauce. There are plenty of combination to choose and play with and if you're really up to trying something old-fashioned and authentic, I would suggest a famous Turkish version of bechamel sauce – Hunkar Begendi. The name itself means "the sultan's treat" and with a reason. This dish is made with eggplant puree and parmesan cheese that are combined together into a creamy sauce that can be used to top different meat dishes or as a lovely Mediterranean replacement to classic mashed potatoes. You will need:

Ingredients

2 large eggplants
½ tsp of freshly squeezed lemon juice
5-6 tbsp of all-purpose flour
¾ cup of butter
½ cup of parmesan cheese
½ cup of warm milk
Salt and pepper to taste

Preparation

1   Grill whole eggplants until the skin begins to break and the pulp feels soft. Remove from the heat and peel. Remove the seeds and place the pulp in a large saucepan. Heat up to a medium heat, add lemon juice and simmer until very soft.

2   Meanwhile, melt the butter. Stir in flour and allow it to brown, stirring constantly. Beat this mixture into the eggplants and slowly add warm milk, stirring constantly.

3   Finish with parmesan cheese, salt, and some pepper.

Eggplant Stew

 **10-15 Minutes**  **4-6 Hours**  **5 Servings**

About Eggplant Stew

Tender and neutral taste of eggplants make them one of the best ingredients in so many different meals. They are easily combined with other foods and perfectly fit every combination. This warm, slow-cooked stew based on eggplants and tomatoes is both – sweet and sour which makes an ideal combination on your plate. Soft eggplants almost melt in your mouth and each bite makes you want more.

Nutritional Information

KCAL	PRT	CARB	FATS
259	7.5g	30g	15.1g

Ingredients

4 medium-sized eggplants, halved
3 large tomatoes, finely chopped
2 red bell peppers, finely chopped
and seeds removed
¼ cup of tomato paste
1 small bunch of fresh parsley, finely
chopped
3.5 oz toasted almonds, finely chopped
2 tbsp of salted capers, rinsed and drained
¼ cup of extra virgin olive oil
1 tsp of sea salt
2 tsp of granulated sugar

Preparation

1. Grease the bottom of a slow cooker with two tablespoons of extra virgin olive oil. Make the first layer with halved eggplants tucking the ends gently to fit in.

2. Now make the second layer with finely chopped tomatoes and red bell peppers. Spread the tomato paste evenly over the vegetables, sprinkle with finely chopped almonds and salted capers. Add the remaining olive oil, salt and pepper.

3. Pour about 1 ½ cups of water and close the lid. Cook for 4-6 hours on low.

Did You Know?

Eggplant - a dark purple, glossy plant comes from India and unlike common belief, it's classified as a fruit, not a vegetable. This magnificent plant was brought to Europe in the 14th century where it gained its popularity. In the 18th century, Thomas Jefferson introduced eggplants to America which is one of the leading producers of this healthy plant today.

Eggplants are not famous for any particular nutrient, but unlike lots of other food, they do contain an impressive amount of many different nutrients making them a real gold mine of health. Just one serving of eggplants will give you a decent amount of fiber, folate, manganese, potassium, vitamins C, K, B6, phosphorus, copper, thiamin, niacin, magnesium, and pantothenic acid. This surely sounds impressive and makes the eggplants number one choice in the kitchen.

Greek Dolmades

 **30 Minutes**    **2-4 Hours**    **5 Servings**

About Greek Dolmades

This recipe takes a while to prepare for cooking but it's definitely worth it! These small, vegan appetizers with fresh wine leaves, rice, and mint are so delicious and refreshing with a traditional spirit of the Mediterranean region. They can be served warm, but they taste so much better when left in the refrigerator overnight. It's up to you!

Nutritional Information

KCAL	PRT	CARB	FATS
313	2.9g	30.4g	20.5g

Ingredients

40 wine leaves, fresh or in jar
1 cup of long grain rice, rinsed
½ cup of olive oil
3 garlic cloves, crushed
¼ cup of freshly squeezed lemon juice
2 tbsp fresh mint
Salt and pepper to taste

Preparation

1   Wash the leaves thoroughly, one at a time. Place on a clean working surface. Grease the bottom of your slow cooker with two tablespoons of olive oil and make a layer with wine leaves. Set aside.

2   In a medium-sized bowl, combine rice with three tablespoons of olive oil, garlic, mint, salt, and pepper. Place one wine leaf at a time on a working surface and add one teaspoon of filling at the bottom end. Fold the leaf over the filling towards the center. Bring the two sides in towards the center and roll them up tightly. Gently transfer to a slow cooker.

3   Add the remaining olive oil, 2 cups of water, and lemon juice. Close the lid and set the heat to low. Cook for 2-4 hours.

4   Remove from the cooker and chill overnight in the refrigerator.

Did You Know?

This lovely Greek dish is traditionally made with cabbage or grape leaves, rice, different herbs, olive oil, and lemon juice. They are usually served cold as an appetizer or a light dinner. Another popular variation of this famous Mediterranean dish includes minced meat (usually beef or pork) and cabbage. They are called Lahanodolmades (Greek cabbage rolls) and are usually served warm as a main course with a traditional egg-lemon sauce called Avgolemono.

Both recipes have dozens of variations and can easily be transformed into vegetarian/meat option. Sprinkle with extra virgin olive oil, fresh lime juice, or a tablespoon of Greek yogurt, and enjoy these lovely bites!

Mediterranean Pizza

 **10 Minutes**  **2 Hours**  **4 Servings**

About Mediterranean Pizza

Who doesn't love a nice, crispy slice of pizza? I guess we all know the answer to that. But did you know that you can prepare a nice homemade pizza in your slow cooker? It sure sounds challenging. Preparing pizza in a slow cooker is really not a big brainer, you simply need to place the dough in it and make the layers with your favorite ingredients. Taking the pizza out of the slow cooker can be somewhat difficult. Make sure to place enough parchment paper under it to ease the process. As simple as that.

Nutritional Information

KCAL	PRT	CARB	FATS
423	12g	30.6g	29.4g

Ingredients

1 standard pizza dough
½ cup of tomato paste
¼ cup of water
1 tsp of sugar
1 tsp of dried oregano
7 oz button mushrooms, sliced
½ cup of grated gouda cheese
2 tbsp of extra virgin olive oil
Olive, sea fennel, arugula, mayonnaise, optional for serving

Preparation

1   Grease the bottom of a slow cooker with one tablespoon of olive oil. Line some parchment paper and set aside. Flour the working surface and roll out the pizza dough to the approximate size of your slow cooker. Gently fit the dough in the cooker.

2   In a small bowl, combine tomato paste with water, sugar, and dry oregano. You can skip this step if you use the pizza sauce. Spread the mixture over dough, make a layer with sliced button mushrooms and grated gouda.

3   Close the lid and set the heat to low. Cook for 2 hours. Gently remove the pizza from your slow cooker using a parchment paper. Sprinkle with the remaining olive oil and optionally top with some olives, mayonnaise, arugula, or even sea fennel for an extra Mediterranean flavor. Cut and serve.

Make It Different

There are probably hundreds of different combinations to prepare pizza. My personal favorite is this Mediterranean style, vegetarian combination. However, it doesn't mean you can't prepare different pizzas in your slow cooker. I want to share probably the most famous version of this traditional Italian dish – pepperoni and cheese pizza. You will need:

Ingredients

One standard pizza dough
3.5 oz sliced pepperoni
3.5 oz grated gouda
2 oz grated parmesan cheese
½ cup of pizza sauce
1 tsp of dried oregano

Preparation

1   Follow the previous recipe to prepare the dough and fit it in your slow cooker. Spread the pizza sauce over it and sprinkle with some dried oregano. Make the first layer with grated gouda, the second layer with sliced pepperoni and finish with grated parmesan cheese. Set the heat to low and cook for two hours.

Patlican Kebab

 **10** Minutes  **4-6** Hours  **5** Servings

About Patlican Kebab

Slowly stewed vegetables with extra virgin olive oil is probably one of the healthiest things you can put on the table. This kebab features tender eggplant and zucchini bites, lightly bitter green bell peppers, soft tomatoes, and a drizzle of melted butter with cayenne pepper. Sprinkle with some finely chopped parsley and serve immediately!

Nutritional Information

KCAL	PRT	CARB	FATS
240	5.1g	29.4g	14.1g

Ingredients

3 medium-sized eggplants, sliced into 1-inch thick slices
1 small zucchini, sliced into 1-inch thick slices
3 large green bell peppers, sliced
2 large tomatoes, finely chopped
2 garlic cloves, crushed
1 tsp of red pepper flakes
½ tsp of freshly ground black pepper
1 tsp of salt
3 tbsp of extra virgin olive oil

Optional Topping

2 tbsp of butter
½ tbsp of cayenne pepper
½ tsp of salt

Preparation

1   Place the sliced vegetables in a greased slow cooker. Add finely chopped tomato, crushed garlic, red pepper flakes, salt, pepper, and one cup of water. Stir well and set the heat to low. Cook for 4-6 hours.

2   When done, remove from the cooker and place on a serving plate. Melt some butter in a small saucepan and add cayenne pepper and salt. Stir-fry for one minute and drizzle over the kebab.

3   Serve immediately.

Did You Know?

Eggplants come from India and Sri Lanka, where it has been grown for more than 3,000. It's amazing healing powers were well known even in ancient times. Today, eggplants are classified as one of the healthiest foods in the world. Its skin is used as a traditional medicine in various cultures of the world as a perfect natural antioxidant, in a prevention of cholesterol, and overall health. For this purpose, you will need 2 large eggplants. Peel the skin and place it in a deep pot. Cover with 5 cups of boiling water and let it stand for about five minutes. Drain the liquid and drink over two or three days.

Babaganoush Recipe

My Middle Eastern travels led me to one of the most famous eggplant recipes in the world 'babaganoush'. I must say that its creamy and soft texture with a gentle touch of spices are definitely worth considering this wonderful recipe every time you want something new at your table. It goes perfectly as a side dish, instead of usual mashed potatoes, or even as a dip with nachos. You will need:

Ingredients

1 lb of eggplants
¼ cup of tahini
1 tbsp of freshly squeezed lemon juice
1 garlic clove, crushed
¼ tsp of salt
¼ cup of fresh parsley, finely chopped

Preparation

1   If using a slow cooker for this recipe, you will have to place the eggplants in a lightly oiled cooker and cover the lid. Gently simmer for 4-6 hours on low. Remove from the cooker and transfer with other ingredients in a food processor. Pulse to combine and keep in jars with a tight lid.

2   Alternatively, bake in the oven for about 20 minutes or grill until fork tender.

Quattro Formaggi Spaghetti

About Quattro Formaggi Spaghetti

Famous Quattro Formaggi sauce can be prepared with so many different cheese types. For this recipe, I have used my favorite ones, but this is totally up to you. Add some heavy cream for extra creaminess and Italian seasoning mix to get the best possible Mediterranean flavor. Sprinkle with grated gouda right before the end and allow it to melt. Enjoy as soon as possible!

Nutritional Information

KCAL	PRT	CARB	FATS
563	25.5g	43.8g	32g

Ingredients

¼ cup of goat's cheese (chevre)
¼ cup of grated Romano cheese
½ cup of grated parmesan
1 cup of heavy cream
½ cup of grated gouda
¼ cup of butter, softened
1 tbsp Italian seasoning mix
1 cup of vegetable broth
½ tsp of salt
1 lb spaghetti noodles

Preparation

1   In a medium-sized bowl, combine goat's cheese with grated Romano cheese, parmesan, and heavy cream. Stir in seasoning and some salt to taste. I personally don't like to add any extra salt, but it's up to you. Transfer to a slow cooker.

2   Stir in the vegetable broth and butter. Close the lid and cook for 2 hours on low.

3   Meanwhile, boil the spaghetti noodles for about 8 minutes (they will cook some more in the slow cooker). Open the cooker's lid and stir in spaghetti. Top with grated gouda and close the lid. Cover and cook for extra 20 minutes on low.

Did You Know?

Quattro formaggi is a term used to describe Italian pasta and pizza with four different types of cheese. The term 'formaggi' itself goes way back into the history to the Roman Empire. When the Romans started to make different hard cheeses for their legionaries, the term 'formaticum, from caseus formatus, or "molded cheese (as in "formed", not "moldy") started to be used. From that term, later on in history, the French fromage, Italian formaggio, Catalan formatge, Breton fourmaj, and Provençal furmo are derived.

Today, quattro formaggi recipes found their ways into many restaurants and homes. A perfect taste of different creamy cheeses is something everybody agrees on. I have decided to spice up this pasta recipe with some Italian seasoning mix based on oregano, basil, and some other herbs. This way you will get a true flavor of Italy in just one warm bowl of spaghetti!

Sour Zucchini Stew

 **10** Minutes  **2-4** Hours  **5** Servings

About Sour Zucchini Stew

Sour zucchini stew is very popular in the Mediterranean region. Traditionally, zucchini and eggplants are combined with tomatoes and sometimes peppers, then slowly stewed over a minimum temperature, and served as a salad. That is exactly what makes this dish perfect for your slow cooker. Add one teaspoon of sugar to adjust the sour taste of this meal and keep in the refrigerator for days.

Nutritional Information

KCAL	PRT	CARB	FATS
132	3.7g	18.1g	6.8g

Ingredients

4 medium-sized zucchini, peeled and sliced
1 large eggplant, peeled and chopped
3 medium-sized red bell peppers
½ cup fresh tomato juice
2 tsp of Italian seasoning
½ tsp of salt
1 tsp of sugar
2 tbsp of olive oil

Preparation

1   Grease the bottom of your cooker with two tablespoons of olive oil. Now add sliced zucchini and eggplant, red bell peppers, and tomato juice. Stir well and season with Italian seasoning, salt, and sugar. Give it a final stir and pour about ½ cup of water.

2   Close the lid and set the heat to low. Cook for 2-4 hours on low. You want the zucchini to be fork tender but not overcooked.

3   Remove from the cooker and keep in the refrigerator. Serve as a cold salad or a side dish.

Did You Know?

Also known as a summer squash, zucchini can grow up to one meter in length, but it is usually harvested while still immature. It belongs to a species Cucurbita pepo with some other squashes and pumpkins. It is considered as a vegetable, but botanically this healthy green plant is actually classified as a fruit. In culinary, zucchini is often combined with other vegetables in some savory meals and side dishes. However, its great nutritive values make zucchini a complete meal. With only 17 calories per 100 grams, with no saturated fats and cholesterol, and plenty of dietary fibers, zucchinis are more than welcome when dealing with weight problems. Their anti-oxidant values are simply remarkable. Zucchinis, especially the golden skin varieties are full of flavonoid poly-phenolic antioxidants like carotenes, lutein and zea-xanthin. These compounds play an important role in slowing down the aging process and fighting off various diseases. And that's not everything to say about zucchinis. Their high amounts of vitamin A, vitamin C, B complex, potassium, and folates are definitely worth mentioning. I bet this will make you fill up a couple of jars with this lovely sour zucchini stew and have your own private stack of these nutrients!

Spinach Pie

 **25 Minutes**  **4-5 Hours**  **5 Servings**

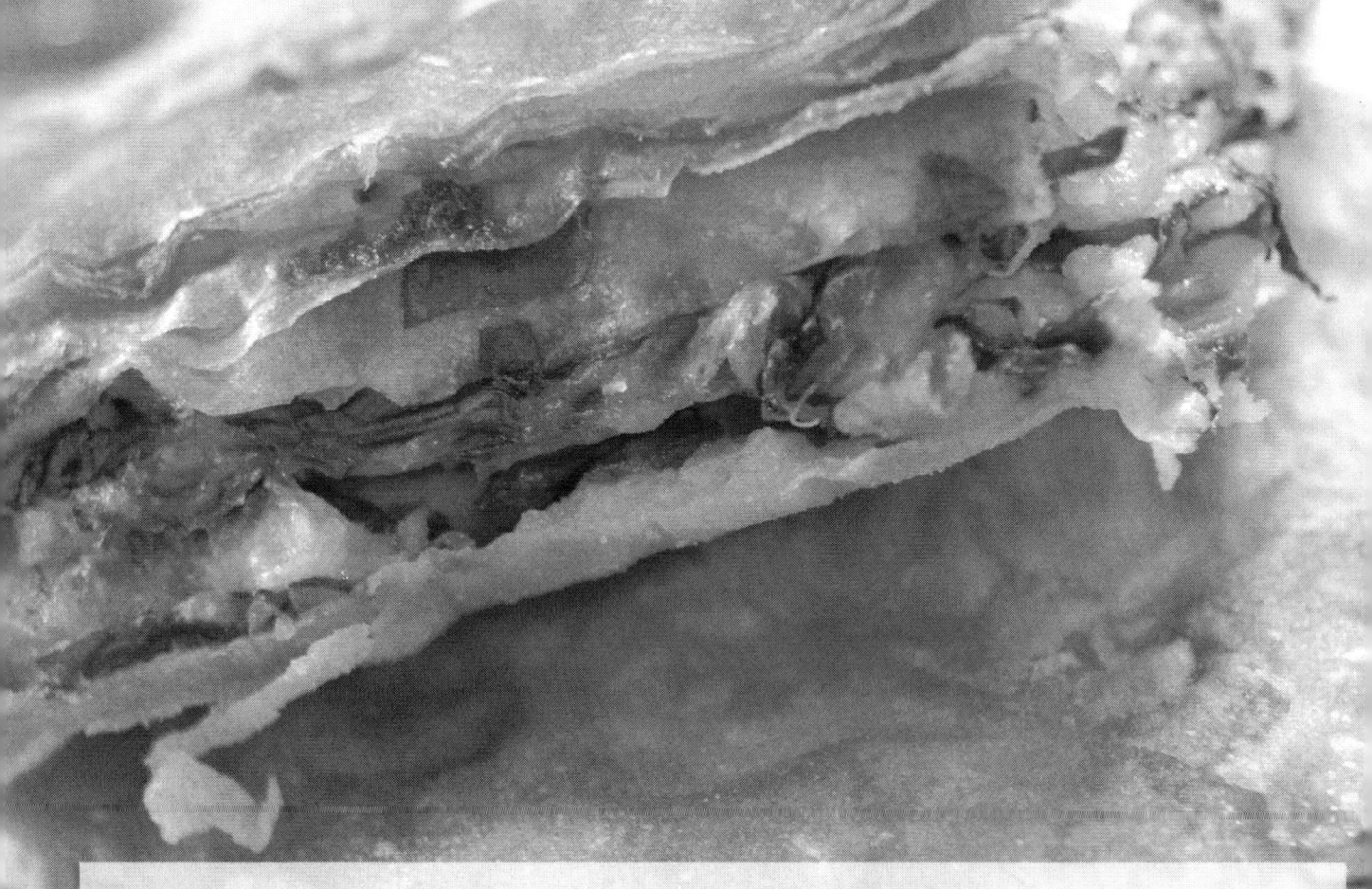

About Spinach Pie

This beautiful Mediterranean-styled spinach pie simply melts in your mouth when you eat it. Its valuable ingredients are more than just a culinary trick. Spinach is one of the healthiest foods on the planet and in this pie, it's combined with protein-rich cheese and eggs creating a satisfying meal.

Nutritional Information

KCAL	PRT	CARB	FATS
297	16.6g	6.6g	23.6g

Ingredients

1 lb spinach, rinsed and finely chopped
½ cup of mascarpone cheese
½ cup feta cheese, shredded
3 eggs, beaten
½ cup of goat's cheese
3 tbsp of butter
½ cup of milk
½ tsp of salt
1 pack (6 sheets) yufka dough
Oil for greasing the cooker

Preparation

1   In a large bowl, combine spinach with eggs, mascarpone, feta, and goat's cheese. Add some salt but be careful because cheese is already salted. Set aside.

2   Dust a clean surface with flour and unfold the sheet of yufka onto it. Using a rolling pin, roll the dough to fit your cooker (I use a 6-quart model). Repeat the process with the remaining five sheets.

3   Combine milk and butter in a small skillet. Bring it to a boil and allow the butter to melt completely. If needed, add some more salt. Remove from the heat.

4   Grease the bottom of your slow cooker with oil. Place two yufka sheets and brush with milk mixture. Make the first layer of spinach mixture and cover with another two yufka sheets. Again, brush with some butter and milk mixture and repeat the process until you have used all the ingredients.

5   Butter and milk will gently soften your yufka dough which is highly recommendable, especially when using a slow cooker. Cover the cooker with a lid and set the heat to low. Cook for 4-5 hours.

6   Removing the pie from a slow cooker can be a bit tricky so you will probably have to cut it while still in the cooker. This, however, can damage your slow cooker. What you can do instead is place some parchment paper under the pie and use it as a lifting method.

Make It Different

I absolutely adore Greek cheese pies. I would like to share with you a recipe that I learned on my travels in Greece. The cooking process is the same as above, but the pie mixture will be slightly different. You will need:

Ingredients

1 cup of feta cheese
1 cup of goat's cheese
1 cup of sour cream
½ cup of heavy cream
5 eggs, beaten
¼ cup of butter, melted
½ cup of milk (or even liquid yogurt)

Preparation

1 Combine the ingredients in a large bowl and use to fill your pie.

Vegetarian Paella

 **5 Minutes**

 **3-4 Hours**

 **4 Servings**

About Vegetarian Paella

For this recipe, you might consider preparing the rice separately. It is almost impossible to prepare it in the slow cooker and not to get a formless sticky mass. However, other ingredients will be ten times better than cooked in any other pot and that is exactly why I wanted to share this recipe. This is a classic Spanish paella but vegetarian-friendly. If you like, you can always stir in a handful of seafood or bite-sized chicken breast. Enjoy!

Nutritional Information

KCAL	PRT	CARB	FATS
235	7.9g	47g	1.4g

Ingredients

½ cup of fresh green peas (frozen will work just fine)
2 small carrots, finely chopped
1 cup of fire-roasted tomatoes
1 cup of zucchini, finely chopped
½ cup of celery root, finely chopped
8 saffron threads
1 tbsp of turmeric, ground
1 tsp of salt
½ tsp of freshly ground black pepper
2 cup of vegetable broth
1 cup of long grain rice

Preparation

1   Place the ingredients, except rice, in a slow cooker. Stir well and cover. Cook for 2 ½ -3 hours on high, until peas are tender.

2   Stir in rice and close the lid. Cook on low for 15-20 more minutes.

3   Optionally, sprinkle with some fresh parsley. Serve warm.

Did You Know?

Paella is a famous rice recipe from Valencia. Its modern form goes back to the 19 century near the Albúfera lagoon (east coast of Spain). This worldwide known dish is considered to be a national Spanish dish, while the Spaniards consider it to be a Valencian dish. However, possible origins of paella go back even further in history, in the times when Moors ruled Spain and began rice cultivation (around the 10th century). It became very popular among the locals who often made rice casseroles with meat, fish, and vegetables. Without knowing it, they established the custom of eating rice in Spain and gave the foundation to this vibrant and fabulous dish. Lourdes March, a famous food historian, said that paella "symbolizes the union and heritage of two important cultures, the Roman, which gives us the utensil and the Arab which brought us the basic food of humanity for centuries."

Fish and Seafood

Black Seafood Pasta

 **15 Minutes**  **6 Hours**  **4 Servings**

About Black Seafood Pasta

Pasta is an important part of the Mediterranean cuisine, but unlike heavy creamy cheese pasta, this lovely seafood recipe will brighten up your day and give some amazing nutritional values to your plate. For this recipe, I used a classic seafood mix, but you can experiment with almost everything that comes from the sea – shrimps, octopus, mussels, or even fish. Whatever you choose, make sure to use the finest olive oil you can find and plenty of garlic because that is exactly what gives this meal its specific taste.

Nutritional Information

KCAL	PRT	CARB	FATS
273	26.1g	3.8g	14.6g

Make It Different

If you're not a big fan of seafood, there is another great option to prepare black pasta with fresh tomatoes, dill, and wine.

Ingredients

1 lb fresh seafood mix
¼ cup of extra virgin olive oil
4 garlic cloves, crushed
1 tbsp of fresh parsley, finely chopped
1 tsp of fresh rosemary, finely chopped
½ cup of white wine
1 tsp of salt
1 lb squid ink pasta

Preparation

1 Grease the bottom of your slow cooker with three tablespoons of olive oil. Add crushed garlic and briefly stir-fry, for 2-3 minutes. Now add seafood mix, fresh parsley, chopped rosemary, and salt. Give it a good stir and add olive oil, whine, and ½ cup of water.

2 Cover, set the heat to low and cook for 6 hours. Use a package instructions to prepare pasta. Squid ink pasta usually doesn't take more than five minutes in a pot of boiling water, so be careful not to overcook it.

3 Open your slow cooker, add cooked pasta, give it a final stir, and serve.

Alternative Ingredients

6-7 medium-sized tomatoes, peeled and roughly chopped (even whole)
4 tbsp of tomato paste
3 large onions, peeled and finely chopped
4 garlic cloves, crushed
3 tbsp of fresh dill, finely chopped
½ cup of white wine
1 cup of water

Alternative Preparation

1 Grease the bottom of your slow cooker with some olive oil and briefly fry the onions, until translucent. Add tomatoes, tomato paste, garlic, dill, white wine, and water. Securely close the lid and cook for 4 hours on low.

Fish Stew

 **15-20 Minutes**  **4-5 Hours**  **6 Servings**

About Fish Stew

Different fish, seafood, and lots of olive oil are three probably most common ingredients in the Mediterranean cuisine. And if you're a fish lover as well, this stew will be something new and totally different, but so healthy and delicious, that you will be making it again and again. The best thing about it is that you can use any fish you have on hand – the more different species, the better!

Nutritional Information

KCAL	PRT	CARB	FATS
504	37.2g	8.1g	35.5g

Ingredients

2 lb of different fish and seafood
¼ cup of extra virgin olive oil
2 large onions, peeled and finely chopped
2 large carrots, grated
A handful of fresh parsley, finely chopped
3 garlic cloves, crushed
3 cups of water (optionally 1 ½ cup of water and 1 ½ cup of dry white wine)
1 tsp of sea salt

Preparation

1 Spread about three tablespoons of olive oil over the bottom of your slow cooker. Add finely chopped onion and crushed garlic. Optionally, you can briefly stir-fry the onions before cooking them for extra flavor, but it's not necessary.

2 Now add the remaining ingredients and close the lid. Set the heat to low and cook for 4-5 hours.

3 Sprinkle with a few drops of freshly squeezed lemon juice before serving, but this is optional.

Make It Different:

Fish soups and stews are very popular in the Mediterranean cuisine and there are various different ways to prepare this lovely fish meal. Besides this classic recipe, I would like to share another one – thick, tomato-based, fish and crab stew. For this recipe, you will need:

Ingredients

2 lb of different fish and crabs
(any other seafood will work perfectly)
1 lb of ripe tomatoes, peeled and roughly chopped
½ cup of extra virgin olive oil
3 cups of water (I like to add 1 ½ cup of dry white wine and 1 ½ cup of water)
A handful of fresh parsley, finely chopped
3 garlic cloves, crushed
2 tbsp of red pepper flakes
2 tsp of dried oregano
1 tsp of sea salt

Preparation

1 Place the ingredients in your slow cooker and simmer for 4 hours on low.

Mackerel with Potatoes

 **20 Minutes**  **6 Hours**  **4 Servings**

About Mackerel with Potatoes

We often forget about this tasty fish, but I promise this amazing slow-cooked mackerel with some potatoes and greens is so good that it will soon become your favorite light summer meal. Serve with some crushed garlic combined with extra virgin olive oil and finely chopped parsley for some extra Mediterranean flavor and enjoy!

Nutritional Information

KCAL	PRT	CARB	FATS
244	14g	19.2g	12g

Ingredients

4 medium-sized mackerels, skin on
1 lb of fresh spinach, torn
5 large potatoes, peeled and sliced
¼ cup (divided in half) of extra virgin olive oil
3 garlic cloves, crushed
1 tsp of dried rosemary, finely chopped
2 springs of fresh mint leaves, chopped
1 lemon, juiced
1 tsp of sea salt

Preparation

1   Peel and slice potatoes. Make the base layer in your slow cooker. Spread one-half of your olive oil over potatoes. Now add torn spinach and top with the remaining olive oil. Add crushed garlic, rosemary, mint, lemon juice, and one cup of water.

2   Generously sprinkle some salt over mackerels. Make the final layer in your slow cooker and close the lid.

3   Cook for 6 hours on low settings or 4 hours on high settings.

Did You Know?

Recent studies have shown that elderly people who frequently consume fish have preserved bone density and are at lower risk of developing osteoporosis. This is related to omega-3 fatty acids, and fish is its best source. It has also been shown that regular fish consumption reduces the risk of colon cancer and rectal cancer by as much as 12 percent. Also, a Mediterranean diet, rich in different fish recipes, prevents the formation of malignant tumors of the reproductive organs.

Wild Salmon with Greens

 **15 Minutes**  **4-5 Hours**  **4 Servings**

About Wild Salmon with Greens

I like salmon in every possible combination, but I believe this is the best one I have ever tasted. Sprinkled with some sea salt (or even Hymalayan salt) it becomes so crispy from the outside, yet so amazingly tender from the inside. Add some healthy spinach as a side dish and enjoy this lovely meal!

Nutritional Information

KCAL	PRT	CARB	FATS
432	44.9g	2.1g	28.3g

Ingredients

1 lb of wild salmon filets, boneless
1 lb of fresh spinach, torn
4 tbsp of olive oil
2 garlic cloves, finely chopped
2 tbsp of lemon juice
1 tbsp of fresh rosemary, chopped
1 tsp of sea salt
¼ tsp of black pepper, ground

Preparation

1   Grease the bottom of a slow cooker with 2 tablespoons of olive oil. Place salmon filets and season with rosemary, salt, and pepper. Drizzle with lemon juice, add about ½ cup of water and cover with a lid. Set the heat to low and cook for 4 hours.

2   Meanwhile, place torn spinach in a large, heavy-bottomed pot. Add enough water to cover and bring it to a boil. Briefly cook, for about two minutes, or until greens are tender. Drain in a colander.

3   After about 4 hours, when the salmon has softened, open the cooker's lid. Remove the salmon from the cooker and place the spinach at the bottom. Add ½ cup of water and garlic. Top with salmon and close the lid again. Cook for 20-30 minutes more and serve.

4   I'm a huge fan of olive oil and I like to sprinkle some more before serving, but this is totally optional.

Did You Know?

Mediterranean's love leafy greens. That's not a secret. They are healthy, tasty, and can be grown in the entire Mediterranean region. The tradition of eating different kinds of leafy greens is so strong that in lots of regions you will still find people growing these vegetables in their gardens and even balconies for one single purpose – to enjoy them most of the year. In the coast of Dalmatia, Herzegovina region, some parts of Italy, Greece and Turkey, the most popular and authentic way to prepare them is to stir-fry torn greens with lots of olive oil and garlic. And when it comes to greens, you can be as creative as you wish. Everything is welcome – spinach, Swiss chard, dandelion, wild asparagus, turnip greens, collards, cabbage, kale, etc. Basically, everything that is green and edible. As simple as that!

CHAPTER SEVEN

Poultry

Chicken Vegetable Stew

 **20 Minutes**

 **8-10 Hours**

 **5 Servings**

About Chicken Vegetable Stew

If you're up for something salty, tender, and extremely tasty, try this rich Mediterranean chicken and vegetable stew. This perfect dish can be made with almost everything you have in the fridge. Experiment with different colors and aromas of fresh vegetables, or even replace the chicken meat with lean beef or veal. Whatever you chose, these aromatic flavors will be something to remember.

Nutritional Information

KCAL	PRT	CARB	FATS
290	31g	39g	6g

Ingredients

1 whole chicken, 3 lbs
10 oz of fresh broccoli
7 oz cauliflower florets
1 large onion, peeled and finely chopped
1 large potato, peeled and chopped
3 medium-sized carrots, sliced
1 large tomato, peeled and chopped
A handful of yellow wax beans, whole
A handful of fresh parsley, finely chopped
¼ cup of extra virgin olive oil
2 tsp of salt
½ tsp of freshly ground black pepper
1 tbsp of cayenne pepper

Preparation

1   Clean the chicken and generously sprinkle with some salt. Set aside.

2   Grease the bottom of your slow cooker with three tablespoons of olive oil. Add finely chopped onion and stir-fry for 3-4 minutes and then add sliced carrot. Continue to cook for five more minutes.

3   Now add the remaining oil, vegetables, salt, black pepper, cayenne pepper, and top with chicken. Add one cup of water and close the lid.

4   Cook for 8-10 hours on low settings.

Make It Vegan

You can easily make a vegan option with this recipe. Simply skip the meat and add something else instead. I like to add ½ cup of pre-cooked green beans, soy beans, white peas, or even chickpeas. It will give this meal some proteins and still taste so perfect. This, however, will reduce the cooking time to 6-7 hours on low setting, or 4 hours on high setting.

Chicken with Green Peppers Stew

 **15 Minutes**  **8 Hours**  **4 Servings**

About Chicken with Green Peppers Stew

Different stewed meat and vegetables are definitely the first thing that comes to mind when we talk about the slow cooker. This wonderful chicken wings and green bell peppers stew is based on tender chicken wings with a tangy taste of green bell peppers. Combined with soft potatoes, sweet carrot, and just one teaspoon of freshly ground chili pepper for an extra kick, this stew truly has a lot to offer.

Nutritional Information

KCAL	PRT	CARB	FATS
325	11.5g	44.5g	12.8g

Ingredients

1 lb chicken breast
2 large potatoes, peeled and finely chopped
5 large green bell peppers, finely chopped and seeds removed
2 small carrots, sliced
2 ½ cups of chicken broth
1 large tomato, roughly chopped
A handful of fresh parsley, finely chopped
3 tbsp of extra virgin olive oil
1 tbsp of cayenne pepper
1 tsp of freshly ground chili pepper
1 tsp of salt

Preparation

1   Grease the slow cooker with three tablespoons of olive oil. Place the vegetables and top with chicken wings. Add chicken broth, one tablespoon of cayenne pepper, salt, and a handful of fresh parsley.

2   Close the lid and set the heat to low. Cook for 8 hours.

Did You Know?

Lovely bell peppers with their glossy exterior that comes in lots of different colors are truly the ornaments of the vegetable world. This healthy plant comes from the same family like potatoes, eggplants, and tomatoes, and it's widely used all over the world in different recipes and spices. Green bell peppers are known for their slightly bitter flavor, while the red and orange bell peppers are sweet.

This lovely plant is an excellent source of more than 30 different members of carotenoid nutrient family making them an admirable source of the vitamin A. And that's not all – bell peppers contain vitamin C and vitamin B6, folate, molybdenum, vitamin E, dietary fiber, vitamin B2, pantothenic acid, niacin, and potassium. All of this makes them an irreplaceable part of your diet.

Chicken with Potatoes

 **15** Minutes    **8-10** Hours    **4** Servings

About Chicken with Potatoes

This is a classic chicken thighs with potatoes dish but with an extra Mediterranean flavored marinade that will give this recipe an extra kick. I like the fresh mint and ginger taste in this marinade, but be careful not to overdo it because you want to keep a nice, crispy chicken taste. Use olive oil for some extra nutrients, serve, and enjoy!

Nutritional Information

KCAL	PRT	CARB	FATS
524	37.8g	45.2g	21.6g

Ingredients

4 chicken thighs, boneless
3 large potatoes, wedged
1 tbsp of freshly squeezed lemon juice
2 garlic cloves, crushed
1 tsp of ginger, ground
1 tbsp of cayenne pepper
1 tsp of fresh mint, finely chopped
¼ cup of olive oil
½ tsp of salt

Preparation

1   In a small bowl, combine olive oil with lemon juice, crushed garlic, ground ginger, mint, cayenne pepper, and salt. Brush each chicken piece with this mixture and transfer to a slow cooker.

2   Add potatoes, the remaining marinade, and 1 ½ cups of water.

3   Close the lid and set the heat to low. Cook for 8-10 hours, or until the potatoes are fork tender.

4   Remove from the cooker and serve warm with some spring onions, but this is optional.

Make It Different:

There are many different Mediterranean-styled marinades you can use to make this recipe special. I personally like this creamy Greek-styled recipe and would like to share it with you. For about 1 lb of chicken thighs, you will need:

Ingredients

1 cup of Greek yogurt
2 oz gorgonzola cheese
1 tsp of finely chopped rosemary
A handful of fresh parsley, finely chopped
¼ cup of extra virgin olive oil
½ tsp of salt

Preparation

1   Combine the ingredients in a bowl and use to brush the chicken before cooking it.

Mushroom Kebab

 **15-20 Minutes**

 **8-9 Hours**

 **4 Servings**

About Mushroom Kebab

This lovely bite-sized kebab made with veal, chicken, mushrooms, and carrots really shows off the luxury of the Mediterranean cuisine. This traditional recipe is full of proteins and combined with carrot for some extra nutrients. Serve with mashed potato, rice, or the authentic hunkar begendi and prepare yourself to amaze everyone at the table!

Nutritional Information

KCAL	PRT	CARB	FATS
373	37.6g	11.3g	20g

Ingredients

1 lb of lean veal cuts, chopped into bite-sized pieces
1 lb of chicken breast, boneless, skinless, and chopped into bite-sized pieces
12 oz button mushrooms, sliced
3 large carrots, sliced
2 tbsp of butter, softened
1 tbsp of olive oil
1 tbsp of cayenne pepper
1 tsp of salt
½ tsp of freshly ground black pepper
A bunch of fresh celery leaves, finely chopped
3.5 oz celery root, finely chopped

Preparation

1   Grease the bottom of your cooker with one tablespoon of olive oil. Now add veal chops, sliced carrot, salt, pepper, cayenne pepper, and celery root. Give it a good stir, add 2 cups of water, and close the lid.

2   Set the heat to low and simmer for 4 hours, or until the meat is half-cooked.

3   Uncover and add chicken breast, butter, and one more cup of water. Continue to simmer for 4 more hours, or until the meat is fully cooked and tender.

4   Finally, add mushrooms and celery. I personally don't like to overcook the mushrooms so about 20 more minutes in the slow cooker will be more than enough.

5   Serve warm.

Did You Know?

Eastern cultures have been celebrating the powerful nutrition benefits of different mushroom species for thousands of years. Mushrooms are often classified with other vegetables and have very few calories per 100 grams. They are totally fat-free, cholesterol-free, gluten-free, very low in sodium, and yet they are extremely rich in some important nutrients like proteins, selenium, potassium, riboflavin, niacin, vitamin D and more.

In the culinary use, they can replace lots of different meat recipes which is perfect for vegetarians and vegans. Their tender taste works perfectly in stews, soups, dressings, combined with meat, fish, vegetable, cheese, or simply sprinkled with spices and grilled. In this recipe, they serve to complete and balance two different types of meat and add some of these amazing nutrients.

Meat

Beef Stew with Eggplants

 -
Minutes

 **8-10 Hours**

 **2 Servings**

About Beef Stew with Eggplants

Rich flavors and valuable nutrients! Those are the first things that come to mind when I think about this heavy eggplant and beef stew. I like to spice things up with some chili pepper, but that is optional. Sprinkle with grated parmesan cheese before serving and enjoy this meal all winter.

Nutritional Information

KCAL	PRT	CARB	FATS
195	15.3g	9.6g	11.1g

Ingredients

10 oz of beef neck, or another tender cut, chopped into bite-sized pieces
1 large eggplant, sliced
2 cups of fire-roasted tomatoes
½ cup of fresh green peas
1 cup of beef broth
4 tbsp of olive oil
2 tbsp of tomato paste
1 tbsp of Cayenne pepper, ground
½ tsp of chili pepper, ground (optional)
½ tsp of salt
Parmesan cheese

Preparation

1   Grease the bottom of a slow cooker with olive oil. Toss all ingredients in it and add about 1-1 ½ cup of water.

2   Cook for 8-10 hours on low, or until the meat is fork-tender.

3   Sprinkle with Parmesan cheese before serving, but this is optional.

Did You Know?

Stews are probably the most popular winter meals worldwide. Their history goes way back to ancient times. The first recorded recipe of this type was written by Greek historian Herodotus. He was writing about Scythians (8th to 4th centuries BC) who used to "put the flesh into an animal's paunch, mix water with it, and boil it like that over the bone fire. The bones burn very well, and the paunch easily contains all the meat once it has been stripped off. In this way an ox, or any other sacrificial beast, is ingeniously made to boil itself." Little did he know that these words were the very first beginning of something that would conquer the culinary world and find its place in many homes in the world.

Chopped Veal Kebab

 **15** Minutes  **8-10** Hours  **5** Servings

About Chopped Veal Kebab

Chopped veal kebab is just one of many different kebab options that are so popular in the entire Mediterranean region. Tender bite-sized veal pieces are slowly cooked and then topped with melted butter, browned cayenne pepper, creamy Greek yogurt, and crispy parsley. Soft pide with melted butter and meat flavor is so delicious that you can't really decide what is tastier — the meat itself or the bread. Try this kebab and see for yourself why this dish is so popular in the entire world.

Nutritional Information

KCAL	PRT	CARB	FATS
437	49.7g	8.9g	21.8g

Ingredients

2 lb boneless veal shoulder, cut into bite-sized pieces
3 large tomatoes, roughly chopped
2 tbsp of all-purpose flour
3 tbsp of butter
1 tbsp of cayenne pepper
1 tsp of salt
1 tbsp of parsley, finely chopped
1 cup of Greek yogurt (can be replaced with sour cream), for serving
1 pide bread (can be replaced with any bread you have on hand)

Preparation

1. Grease the bottom of your slow cooker with one tablespoon of butter. Make a layer with veal chops and pour enough water to cover. Season with salt and close the lid.

2. Set the heat to low and simmer for 8-10 hours.

3. When the meat is fork tender, remove from the slow cooker and transfer to a plate.

4. Melt the remaining butter in a small skillet. Add one tablespoon of cayenne pepper, two tablespoons of all-purpose flour, and briefly stir-fry - for about two minutes. Remove from the heat.

5. Chop pide bread and arrange on a serving plate. Place the meat and tomato on top. Drizzle with browned cayenne pepper, top with Greek yogurt and sprinkle with chopped parsley.

6. Serve immediately.

Did You Know?

Kebab is a term used to describe a wide variety of meat recipes combined with grilled vegetables and different spices. Many kebabs include a small, bite-sized pieces of meat on skewers. However, there are countless different types of kebabs and they include almost everything – from different meat pieces, seafood, fish, vegetables, and spices to different ways of preparing them like grilling, cooking as a stew, roasting over the fire, frying, and even baking in the oven. This recipe is a classic veal kebab but more tender because it has been slow cooked. Make sure to top with some creamy yogurt for extra flavor.

Garlic Meatballs

 **20 Minutes**  **6-8 Hours**  **4-5 Servings**

About Garlic Meatballs

Lovely garlic meatballs are a perfect way to enjoy a warm meal at the end of a day. This typical Mediterranean meal combined with rice, onions, and the smallest amount of garlic is so easy to prepare and will soon become one of your slow-cooker favorites. Replace the usual butter with some olive oil for extra nutrients and enjoy this culinary delight when you get home from work.

Nutritional Information

KCAL	PRT	CARB	FATS
468	33g	47g	15.3g

Ingredients

1 lb lean ground beef
7 oz rice
2 small onions, peeled and finely chopped
2 garlic cloves, crushed
1 egg, beaten
1 large potato, peeled and sliced
3 tbsp of extra virgin olive oil
1 tsp of salt

Preparation

1   In a large bowl, combine lean ground beef with rice, finely chopped onions, crushed garlic, one beaten egg, and salt. Shape the mixture into 15-20 meatballs, depending on the size.

2   Grease the bottom of your slow cooker with three tablespoons of olive oil. Make the first layer with slice potatoes and top with meatballs.

3   Cover, set the heat to low and cook for 6-8 hours.

Did You Know?

Mediterranean meatballs are also known as kofte. Traditionally, they're made with minced beef, pork, chicken, and lamb; onions, and some spices. In some parts of Greece, fish meatballs are very popular, while in Europe they are served as fast food in a form of kebab.

There are so many variations of this popular dish. The meat is mixed with rice, potato puree, bulgur, different vegetables, and spices; then cooked, fried, or even baked. This really gives you a plenty of options to combine and find your own favorite recipe. You can serve these lovely meatballs as a main dish, an appetizer, a side dish, or even a snack. Whatever you choose, meatballs will fit in.

Meat Pie with Yogurt

 **20** Minutes

 **4-6** Hours

 **6** Servings

About Meat Pie with Yogurt

Creamy meat pie with yogurt is served cold as a lovely appetizer or a main dish. This lovely Mediterranean dish is based on lean ground beef, garlic, and topped with creamy yogurt. Can stand in the refrigerator for days and taste even better than the first day. Sprinkle with some red pepper before serving and you're good to go.

Nutritional Information

KCAL	PRT	CARB	FATS
503	47.4g	2.6g	32.8g

Ingredients

2 lb lean ground beef
5-6 garlic cloves, crushed
1 tsp of salt
½ tsp freshly ground black pepper
1 (16 oz) pack yufka dough
½ cup of butter, melted
1 cup of sour cream
3 cups of liquid yogurt

Preparation

1   In a large bowl, combine ground beef with garlic cloves, salt, and pepper. Mix well until fully incorporated.

2   Lay a sheet of yufka on a work surface and brush with melted butter. Line with the meat mixture and roll up. Repeat the process until you have used all the ingredients.

3   Gently place in a lightly greased slow cooker and close the lid. Cook for 4-6 hours on low, remove from the cooker and allow it to cool. Meanwhile, combine sour cream with yogurt. Spread the mixture over pie and serve cold.

Make It Different:

This pie can be filled with many different combinations. The recipe above is the most common and a traditional way to prepare this meal. However, you can easily turn this pie into a lovely vegetarian dish. For this recipe, you will need:

Ingredients

1 lb mashed potatoes
7 oz sour cream
1 tsp salt

Preparation

1   Combine the ingredients in a large bowl and use to fill the pie. Follow the recipe and enjoy with or without the yogurt topping.

Moussaka

 **15** Minutes  **8** Hours  **5** Servings

About Moussaka

Three layers of pure culinary perfection! Another great Mediterranean meal that comes in so many different forms which is probably the best thing about it. Replace potatoes with zucchini or eggplants, add a slice of cheese between layers, or one tablespoon of tomato paste; and you have an entirely new recipe. This simple lean ground beef and potato moussaka is both – tender and crispy with creamy yogurt topping. I promise you will love this one!

Nutritional Information

KCAL	PRT	CARB	FATS
458	34.9g	36g	19.2g

Ingredients

2 lb large potatoes, peeled and sliced
1 lb lean ground beef
1 large onion, peeled and finely chopped
1 tsp of salt
½ tsp of black pepper, ground
½ cup of milk
2 large eggs, beaten
Vegetable oil
Sour cream or Greek yogurt, for serving

Preparation

1. Grease the bottom of your cooker with some vegetable oil. Make one layer with sliced potatoes and brush with some milk. Spread the ground beef and make another layer with potatoes. Brush well with the remaining milk, add ½ cup of water, and close the lid.

2. Cook for 8 hours on low, or 4-6 hours on high.

3. When done, make the final layer with beaten egg. Cover the cooker and let it stand for about 10 minutes.

4. Top with some sour cream or Greek yogurt and serve!

Did You Know?

Moussaka is a potato, eggplant, and/or zucchini based dish with a layer of ground beef. The origins of this Mediterranean meal go back to the former Ottoman Empire with many regional variations. It is often served warm, directly from the oven, as a casserole. Some regions prepare this dish only with eggplants and refrigerate it overnight, which is also a great idea, especially when topped with cream cheese, sour cream, or yogurt. In Greece, for example, moussaka is served with milk-based custard, or bechamel sauce, while in Turkey, moussaka doesn't even include layers but rather sauteed eggplants with ground beef. Balkan countries prefer two layers of potato with ground beef (or pork) in the middle. Honestly, I can't decide which recipe tastes better – I guess they all have their own special charm and it's up to you to discover your own favorite recipe.

Pepper Meat

 **20** Minutes  **8-10** Hours  **6** Servings

About Pepper Meat

The name itself says that you're about to prepare one spicy and piquant dish. It requires tender meat pieces, lots of onions, and pepper which can be freshly ground black pepper, mixed pepper, or white pepper. This combination works perfect for my taste, however, if you really want to give it a special kick, stir in a pinch of chili pepper. Serve with my favorite saffron rice and enjoy this meal!

Nutritional Information

KCAL	PRT	CARB	FATS
382	47.3g	10.3g	16g

Ingredients

2 lbs of beef fillet or another tender cut
5 medium-sized onions, peeled and finely chopped
3 tbsp of tomato paste
2 tbsp of oil
1 tbsp of butter, melted
2 tbsp of fresh parsley, finely chopped
½ tsp of freshly ground black pepper
1 tsp of salt

Preparation

1   Grease the bottom of your slow cooker with some oil. About two tablespoons will be enough.

2   Cut the meat into a bite-sized pieces and place in the cooker. Add finely chopped onions, tomato paste, fresh parsley, salt, and pepper. Give it a good stir and add about 2 cups of water.

3   Close the lid and set the heat to low. Cook for 8-10 hours.

4   When done (the meat should be fork tender), stir in one tablespoon of melted butter and serve warm.

Did You Know?

Eggplants come from India and Sri Lanka, where it has been grown for more than 3,000. It's amazing healing powers were well known even in ancient times. Today, eggplants are classified as one of the healthiest foods in the world. Its skin is used as a traditional medicine in various cultures of the world as a perfect natural antioxidant, in a prevention of cholesterol, and overall health. For this purpose, you will need 2 large eggplants. Peel the skin and place it in a deep pot. Cover with 5 cups of boiling water and let it stand for about five minutes. Drain the liquid and drink over two or three days.

Optional Serving

Pepper meat goes with pretty much everything — mashed or boiled potatoes, french fries, rice, pasta, or with pide bread. But I would like to share with you one of my favorite side dishes for this amazing meat recipe — saffron rice.

Ingredients

1 cup of Basmati rice
3 cups of vegetable broth
½ tsp of saffron threads
1 tsp of ground turmeric
2 tbsp of extra virgin olive oil
Salt and pepper to taste
¼ cup of dry white wine (optionally)

Preparation

1   Place rice in a deep heavy-bottomed pot and pour the vegetable broth. Give it a good stir and bring it to a boil. Reduce the heat and stir in turmeric, olive oil, saffron, and some salt and pepper. Cook for about 12-15 minutes, or until all the liquid has evaporated. Optionally, you can add about ¼ cup of white wine.

2   This simple recipe can also be prepared in your slow cooker. In that case, rub your slow cooker with olive oil. Place all other ingredients and close the lid. Cook for 2 hours on high. Stir in the wine right before serving, but this is optional.

Roast Lamb

 **10 Minutes**

 **7-8 Hours**

 **5 Servings**

About Roast Lamb

This slow cooked lamb recipe is crispy and tender at the same time and a perfect option when you're in the mood for a true culinary delight. Full of proteins, rich looking, with a taste that everybody enjoys, this classic roast lamb recipe can be even better when prepared on a Mediterranean way with melted butter, pide bread, and fresh vegetables. Serve and enjoy!

Nutritional Information

KCAL	PRT	CARB	FATS
473	49.7g	8.9g	21.8g

Ingredients

2 lb lamb leg
3 tbsp extra virgin olive oil
2 tsp salt

Preparation

1   Grease the bottom of a slow cooker with three tablespoons of olive oil. Rinse and generously season the meat with salt and place in the cooker. Close the lid and set the heat to low. Cook for one hour on high and 6-7 hours on low, or until the meat is tender and separates from the bones.

Optional Serving

Melted butter with salt or even one tablespoon of cayenne pepper will add some extra calories to your meal, but the taste will be so much better that you won't regret it. This butter topping is typical for the Mediterranean cuisine, especially different kebabs, but works perfectly in many other recipes, especially meat. Give it a try:

Ingredients

3 tbsp butter
1 tsp sea salt
¼ cup fresh parsley, finely chopped
1 medium-sized onion, peeled and sliced
1 small tomato, roughly chopped
Pita bread (fougasse, or any other flattened bread you can get)

Preparation

1   Arrange the meat, bread, sliced onion, and tomato on a serving plate.

2   Melt three tablespoons of butter in a small skillet. Add one teaspoon of sea salt and briefly stir-fry for one minute. Remove from the heat and pour over bread and meat. Sprinkle with fresh parsley, maybe add a couple of olives and serve.

Rosemary Meatballs

 **20-25 Minutes**

 **4-6 Hours**

 **4 Servings**

About Rosemary Meatballs

Rosemary meatballs with lean ground beef and garlic is a Mediterranean classic that is usually served with spaghetti, tomato, or a yogurt sauce. These crispy bites can be eaten in so many different ways. I personally like to serve them as a cold appetizer topped with some creamy yogurt with parsley and garlic. They can stand in the refrigerator for days which makes them a perfect option for holidays. Enjoy!

Nutritional Information

KCAL	PRT	CARB	FATS
477	49g	17.8g	21.4g

Ingredients

1 lb lean ground beef
3 garlic cloves, crushed
¼ cup of all-purpose flour
1 tbsp of fresh rosemary, crushed
1 large egg, beaten
½ tsp of salt
3 tbsp of extra virgin olive oil

For Serving

2 cups of liquid yogurt
1 cup of Greek yogurt
2 tbsp of fresh parsley
1 garlic clove, crushed

Preparation

1   In a large bowl, combine ground beef with crushed garlic, rosemary, one egg, and salt. Using a spoon or your hands, mix well to combine. I like to add some corn flour for extra crispiness, but this is totally optional.

2   Lightly dampen hands and shape 1 ½ inch balls transferring into greased cooker as you work. Slowly add about ½ cup of water. Close the lid and set the heat to low. Cook for 4-6 hours.

3   Remove from the cooker and cool completely. Meanwhile, combine liquid yogurt with Greek yogurt, parsley, and crushed garlic. Stir well and drizzle over meatballs.

Did You Know?

Rosemary is a typical Mediterranean spice with many proven health benefits. It's amazing healing powers and the extreme benefits of its essential oils are known since the ancient times. Locals used this herb to improve memory, intelligence, and focus. Today, these effects are a subject of many studies which prove rosemary to increase a memory retention, to stimulate cognitive activity in the elderly population, and to help reduce the effects of acute cognitive disorders. One of the most powerful health benefits rosemary has is its ability to reduce the consequences of Alzheimer's disease. This amazing herb also has the amazing effect on our entire immune system. The active components found in it have constant antioxidant, anti-inflammatory, anti-carcinogenic activity, and a huge anti-bacterial potential.

Being a home to this amazing herb resulted in extensive use of rosemary in so many different regional cuisines and recipes. It's almost impossible to find a good grilled fish recipe without it. Fresh and dried rosemary are unreplaceable in stews; chicken, veal, and beef recipes; dressings, marinades, seafood salads, and much more. Finely chopped rosemary is used to prepare the famous Italian focaccia.

An old saying in the Dalmatian region goes "One of few unforgivable sins before god is to use dried instead of fresh rosemary". Believe it or not, one thing is for sure – fresh rosemary will instantly bring the vibrant taste of the Mediterranean cuisine directly to your table. Enjoy it!

Spicy White Peas

 **10 Minutes**  **8-9 Hours**  **4 Servings**

About Spicy White Peas

Warm chili peas with slices of bacon is one of the best meals you can prepare in your slow cooker. This meal was traditionally prepared on an open fire and cooked for 24 hours. This way it gets to keep every single drop of taste you can possibly imagine. This way of cooking today is very inconvenient, almost impossible. The slow cooker is the best possible option to replace the traditional way of preparing this unbelievable meal. Simply throw the ingredients in it and enjoy!

Nutritional Information

KCAL	PRT	CARB	FATS
210	4g	24g	12g

Ingredients

1 lb of white peas
4 slices of bacon
1 large onion, finely chopped
1 small chili pepper, finely chopped
2 tbsp of all-purpose flour
2 tbsp of butter
1 tbsp of cayenne pepper
3 bay leaves, dried
1 tsp of salt
½ tsp of freshly ground black pepper

Preparation

1   Melt two tablespoons of butter in a slow cooker. Add chopped onion and stir well. Now add bacon, peas, finely chopped chili pepper, bay leaves, salt, and pepper. Gently stir in two tablespoons of flour and add three cups of water.

2   Securely close the lid and cook for 8-9 hours on low setting or 5 hours on high setting.

Make It Greek

Another great way to use your slow cooker is to make a perfect Greek-style white beans in tomato sauce. For this lovely recipe you will need:

Ingredients

1 lb of white beans
2 large tomatoes, peeled and chopped
2 garlic cloves, crushed
½ cup of extra virgin olive oil
A handful of fresh parsley, finely chopped
¼ cup of tomato paste

Preparation

1   Simply combine the ingredients in a slow cooker. Add one cup of water and close the lid. Set the heat to low and cook for 8 hours.

Stuffed Collard Greens

 **30 Minutes**  **4 Hours** **5 Servings**

About Stuffed Collard Greens

To make this lovely Mediterranean dish you will need collard greens. It is considered to be one of the healthiest foods in the world and with a good reason – it contains a true gold mine of vitamins and minerals.

The taste of ground beef in this meal is really special and can easily be combined with some dried meat for extra flavor. You can serve it warm or cold, with or without a side dish, but whatever you chose, these lovely Mediterranean rolls will bring a true Mediterranean spirit at your dining table.

Nutritional Information

KCAL	PRT	CARB	FATS
156	5.2g	21g	7g

Ingredients

1.5 lb of collard greens, steamed
1 lb lean ground beef
2 small onions, peeled and finely chopped
½ cup long grain rice
2 tbsp of olive oil
1 tsp of salt
½ tsp of freshly ground black pepper
1 tsp of mint leaves, finely chopped

Preparation

1. Boil a large pot of water and gently the greens. Briefly cook, for 2-3 minutes. Drain and gently squeeze the greens and set aside.

2. In a large bowl, combine the ground beef with finely chopped onions, rice, salt, pepper, and mint leaves.

3. Oil the slow cooker with some olive oil. Place leaves on your work surface, vein side up. Use one tablespoon of the meat mixture and place it in the bottom center of each leaf. Fold the sides over and roll up tightly. Tuck in the sides and gently transfer to a slow cooker.

4. Cover and cook on low setting for ten hours, or on high setting for 4 hours.

Optional Serving

I have decided to serve my collard greens with some mashed potatoes and tomato sauce. This, of course, is optional. However, fresh tomato sauce will give you some extra Mediterranean flavor. You will need:

Mashed Potatoes

4 large potatoes, peeled and sliced
½ cup of milk
½ tsp of salt
3 tbsp of butter

Tomato Sauce

4 medium-sized tomatoes, peeled and finely chopped
1 tsp of sugar
½ tsp of salt
¼ cup of white wine
1 tbsp of extra virgin olive oil
1 tbsp of butter
½ tsp of dry oregano

Preparation

1 First, you will have to peel and slice potatoes into 1 inch thick slices. Wash, rinse and place in a deep pot. Add enough water to cover and bring it to a boil. Cook until fork tender and remove from the heat. Add ½ tsp of salt, lukewarm milk, and butter. Using a potato masher or electric beater, blend the mixture until smooth and creamy.

2 Oil a large skillet with some olive oil. Melt the butter and add finely chopped tomatoes. Give it a good stir and add salt, sugar, wine, and oregano. Simmer for ten minutes, stirring occasionally. Remove from the heat and serve warm.

Stuffed Onions

 **20 Minutes**  **6-8 Hours**  **5 Servings**

About Stuffed Onions

Tender sweet onions stuffed with lean ground beef and some traditional spices are truly impressive side dish or even a main course. Serve warm with pide bread, sour cream and its own tomato sauce. Optionally sprinkle with some fresh parsley or arugula and enjoy this lovely Mediterranean dish.

Nutritional Information

KCAL	PRT	CARB	FATS
464	34g	48.4g	15.2g

Ingredients

10-12 medium-sized sweet onions, peeled
1 lb of lean ground beef
½ cup of rice
3 tbsp of olive oil
1 tbsp of dry mint, ground
1 tsp of Cayenne pepper, ground
½ tsp of cumin, ground
1 tsp of salt
½ cup of tomato paste
½ cup Italian-style bread crumbs
A handful of fresh parsley, finely chopped

Preparation

1   Cut a ¼-inch slice from top of each onion and trim a small amount from the bottom end, This will make the onions stand upright. Place onions in a microwave-safe dish and add about one cup of water. Cover with a tight lid and microwave on HIGH 10 to 12 minutes or until onions are tender. Remove onions from a dish and cool slightly. Now carefully remove inner layers of onions with paring knife, leaving about a ¼-inch onion shell.

2   In a large bowl, combine ground beef with rice, olive oil, mint, cayenne pepper, cumin, salt, and bread crumbs. Use one tablespoon of the mixture to fill the onions.

3   Grease the bottom of a slow cooker with some oil and add onions. Add about 2 ½ cups of water and cover. Cook for 6-8 hours on low setting.

4   Sprinkle with chopped parsley or even arugula and serve with sour cream and pide bread.

Did You Know?

Health benefits of onions are not a brainer, but did you know that recent studies had shown that a moderate consumption of onions prevents several different types of cancer – including esophageal cancer and cancers of the mouth. But what is a proper amount we should eat in order to get this amazing 'side-effect' of onions? Well, the answer lies in the Mediterranean diet! We all have to agree that a handful of sliced onions in a salad is a good thing, but not enough to provide these specific benefits. Mediterranean recipes, on the other hand, are almost impossible without onions. With this type of diet, you will be eating generous amounts of this superb vegetable every single day. And what's more fascinating – the meals are so tasty that will make you want to enjoy them all year round!

Stuffed Peppers

 **25 Minutes**

 **6 Hours**

 **4 Servings**

About Stuffed Peppers

Stuffed peppers are one of the best ways to get creative with food. In the Mediterranean region, you can find countless of different combination to fill your peppers. I have decided to share with you this classic ground beef recipe typical for Moroccan, Turkish, and Greek cuisine. For a vegetarian version, simply combine different vegetables and use to fill peppers. Serve and enjoy!

Nutritional Information

KCAL	PRT	CARB	FATS
410	37.9g	24.7g	18.2g

Ingredients

2 lbs of green peppers
1 large onion, finely chopped
1 lb of lean ground beef
¼ cup of rice
½ cup of fire roasted tomatoes
1 medium-sized tomato, sliced
½ tsp of salt
1 tsp of cayenne pepper
3 tbsp of olive oil

Preparation

1   Cut the stem end of each pepper and remove the seeds. Rinse and set aside.

2   In a medium-sized bowl, combine meat with finely chopped onion, rice, tomatoes, salt, and cayenne pepper. Stir well to combine. Use about 1-2 tablespoons of this mixture and fill each pepper, but make sure to leave at least ½ inch of headspace.

3   Grease the bottom of your slow cooker with some oil. Make the first layer with tomato slices. Gently arrange the peppers and add two cups of water. Optionally, toss in a handful of green beans and close the lid. Cook for 6 hours on low.

Make It Different

What I like about this recipe is that you can make it new and exciting every time you make it. For a simple vegetarian option, you will need:

Ingredients

1 large eggplant, peeled and finely chopped
2 medium-sized bell peppers, finely chopped and seeds removed
¼ cup of rice
¼ cup of fire-roasted tomatoes
6 saffron threads
1 tbsp of cayenne pepper
1 tsp of salt
3 tbsp of extra virgin olive oil

Preparation

1   Combine the ingredients in a bowl and use the mixture to stuff peppers. Optionally, top with some Greek yogurt or sour cream and serve.

Veal Okra

 **15-20** Minutes  **8-10** Hours  **4** Servings

About Veal Okra

This luxurious meal tastes even better than it looks. Nicely trimmed fresh okra perfectly absorbs the flavors of tender veal chops and bittersweet tomatoes. The taste is completed with soft Jerusalem artichokes, crispy cauliflower florets, and healthy broccoli. Sprinkle with some fresh lemon juice right before serving and enjoy this Mediterranean delight!

Nutritional Information

KCAL	PRT	CARB	FATS
281	19.6g	17.4g	15.5g

Ingredients

7 oz veal shoulder, blade chops
1 lb okra, rinsed and trimmed
3 large Jerusalem artichokes, whole
2 medium-sized tomatoes, halved
2-3 fresh cauliflower florets
2 cups of vegetable broth
A handful of fresh broccoli
3 tablespoons of extra virgin olive oil
1 tsp of Himalayan salt
½ tsp of freshly ground black pepper

Preparation

1 Grease your slow cooker with three tablespoons of olive oil. Set aside.

2 Cut each okra pod in half lengthwise and place in a slow cooker. Add tomato halves, Jerusalem artichokes, cauliflower florets, a handful of fresh broccoli, and top with meat chops.

3 Season with salt and pepper and add two cups of vegetable broth. Give it a good stir and close the lid.

4 Set the heat to low and cook for 8-10 hours.

Did You Know?

Jerusalem artichoke is also known as the earth apple, sunroot, sunchoke, and topinambour. This magnificent plant is native to North America and can be eaten raw or cooked. Their amazing nutritional values and almost neutral taste make them one of the best health boosting additions to different stews, soups, and salads. These potato-like plants contain plenty of inulin which makes them extremely powerful prebiotics. Besides their prebiotic properties, Jerusalem artichokes are packed with B vitamins (especially Thiamine), potassium, and iron. With only 73 calories per 100 grams and totally fat-free, this plant is truly a valuable addition to this recipe.

Winter Lamb Stew

 **15 Minutes**

 **10 Hours**

 **4 Servings**

About Winter Lamb Stew

A warm bowl of tender lamb that melts in your mouth combined with soft potatoes, carrots, and bittersweet tomatoes is exactly what you need on a cold winter's day. Add one garlic head to keep the authenticity of the recipe and enjoy!

Nutritional Information

KCAL	PRT	CARB	FATS
379	34.6g	24.2g	15.7g

Ingredients

1 lb of lamb neck, boneless
2 medium-sized potatoes, peeled
and chopped into bite-sized pieces
2 large carrots, sliced
1 medium-sized tomato, diced
1 small red bell pepper, chopped
1 garlic head, whole
A handful of fresh parsley, finely chopped
2 tbsp of extra virgin olive oil
¼ cup of lemon juice
½ tsp of salt
½ tsp of black pepper, ground

Preparation

1   Grease the bottom of a slow cooker with olive oil.

2   Place the meat at the bottom of the cooker and season with salt. Now add the other ingredients, tuck in one garlic head in the middle of the pot and add 2 cups of water (you can use a vegetable broth instead, but this is optional).

3   Add a handful of fresh parsley and close the lid. Set the heat to low and simmer for 10 hours.

Did You Know?

This is a traditional meal from the Balkan region. It is said that the best way to prepare this lamb stew is over an open fire for 24 hours! For centuries, this recipe was prepared in old-fashioned clay pots sealed with parchment and secured with a wire. Unfortunately, most of us don't have the opportunity to prepare this lovely winter stew like this, but it is exactly what makes this colorful lamb meal a perfect option for your slow cooker!

Desserts

Apple Pie

About Apple Pie

I absolutely adore a good homemade apple pie! For me, it is a true sign of autumn when I gather my family and we go out in the garden and pick apples directly from the trees. This year I have decided to add some extra nutritional values to my classic pie recipe – flax seed. It has a neutral taste, it's crunchy, and really goes great with everything! Enjoy!

Nutritional Information

KCAL	PRT	CARB	FATS
214	2.8g	27.4g	11g

Ingredients

2 pounds of apples (I used Zestar apples, but you can really use any kind of apples you have on hand)

¼ cup of granulated sugar

¼ cup of breadcrumbs

2 tsp of cinnamon, ground

3 tbsp of freshly squeezed lemon juice

1 tsp of vanilla sugar

¼ cup of oil

1 egg, beaten

¼ cup of all-purpose flour

2 tbsp of flax seed

Pie dough

Preparation

1 First, peel the apples and cut into bite- sized pieces. Transfer to a large bowl. I like to add about two to three tablespoons of freshly squeezed lemon juice. It gives my pie a nice sour flavor and it prevents the apples to change the color before cooking. Now add breadcrumbs, vanilla sugar, granulated sugar, and cinnamon. You can also add one teaspoon of ground nutmeg in the mixture. I personally avoid it because I like the classic cinnamon taste. But you can experiment a bit. Mix well the ingredients and set aside.

2 On a lightly floured surface roll out the pie dough making 2 circle-shaped crusts. Grease the slow cooker with some oil (or even melted butter) and place one pie crust in it. Spoon the apple mixture and cover with the remaining crust. Seal by crimping edges and brush with beaten egg.

3 I like to sprinkle my pie with flax seed. It adds some great nutritional values to it, but it also gives a bit of crunchy flavor I absolutely adore. This, however, is optional. You can sprinkle your pie with some nice powdered sugar instead. That really depends on your taste.

4 Cover, set the heat to low and cook for 7 hours.

Make Your Own Pie Dough!

If you have some spare time and you want to play with your own apple pie dough, the recipe is really simple. You will need:

Ingredients

1 lb all-purpose flour plus ½ cup for rolling dough
1 cup of lukewarm water
½ tsp of salt
2 tbsp of sugar
1 tbsp of apple cider vinegar
¼ cup of oil plus 2 tbsp

Preparation

1   In a large bowl, combine 1lb of flour with salt and sugar. Mix well with a spoon. Now slowly add lukewarm water, oil, and cider. I always add some apple cider vinegar in the dough because it gives an amazing crispness to my pie. This old trick is perfect for every pie recipe. Now you want to beat your ingredients well on high until dough holds together when squeezed with fingers. Place the dough on a lightly floured working surface and form 1 inch thick discs. Wrap tightly in plastic and keep in a warm place for about an hour.

2   After about an hour, unwrap the dough and roll out into circle shaped pie crusts. This should give you four pie crusts. Use two for your apple pie and wrap the other two in plastic. Keep in the freezer until the next time.

Classic French Squash Pie

 **15** Minutes  **4** Hours  **8** Servings

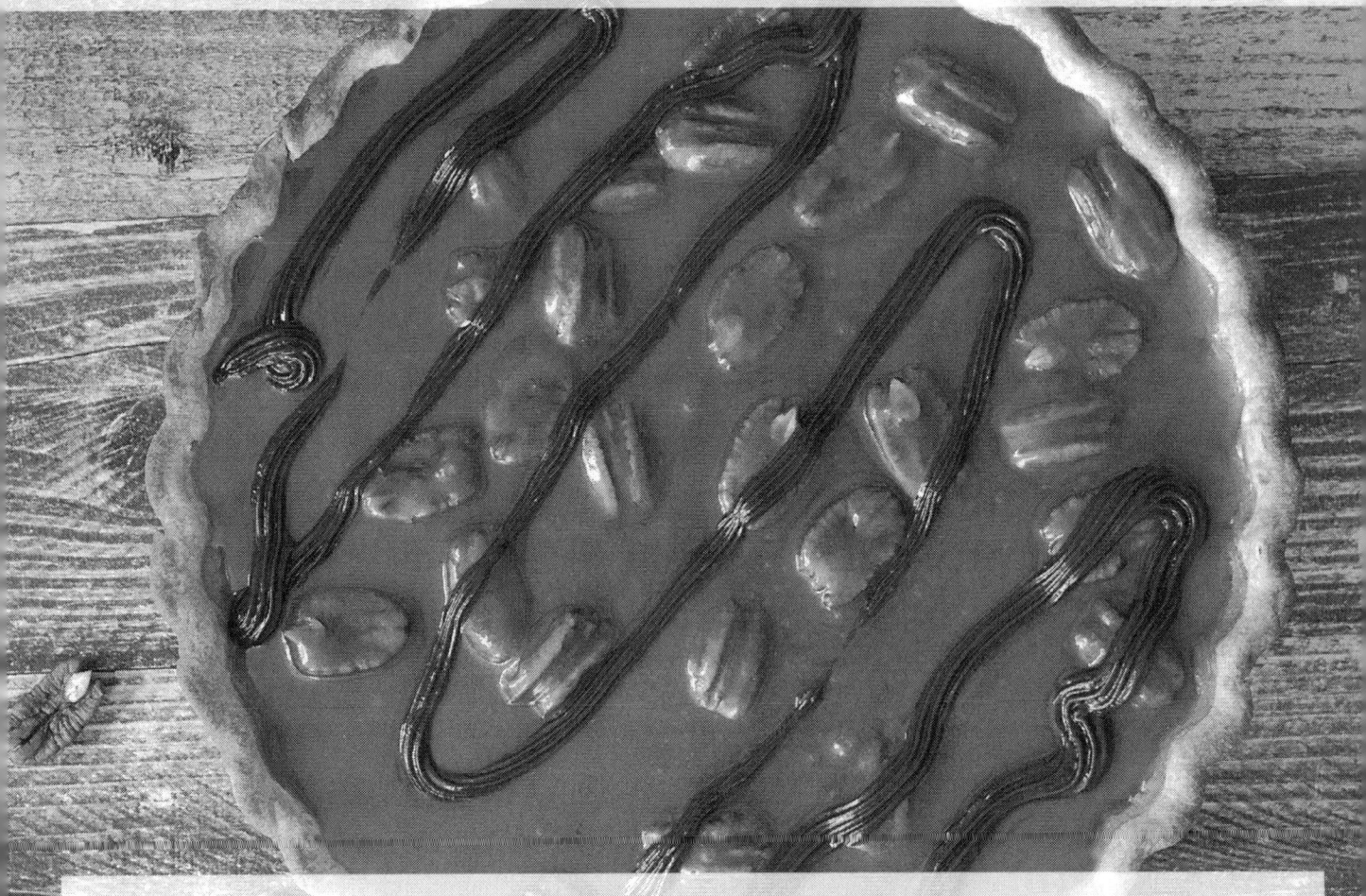

About Classic French Squash Pie

Pumpkin was one of the first foods that European explorers brought back from the New World. It dates back to 1536 when they were called "pumpions," after the French "pompon," because of they rounded shape. Pumpkins quickly gained enormous popularity in whole Europe. In 1653 French cookbooks instructed chefs to boil the pumpkin in milk and then mash it before putting it in a crust. This one is a classic squash pie recipe with milk and nutmeg with amazing French patee brisee that you can buy in a store or even make your own within minutes. Let's dig a little deeper in amazing French cuisine.

Nutritional Information

KCAL	PRT	CARB	FATS
188	7g	51g	16g

Ingredients

15 oz mashed squash
6 fl oz whole milk
½ tsp of cinnamon, ground
½ tsp of nutmeg
½ tsp of salt
3 large eggs
½ cup of granulated sugar
1 pack of pate brisee

Preparation

1   Place squash puree in a large bowl.

2   Now add milk, cinnamon, eggs, nutmeg, salt, and sugar. Whisk together until well incorporated.

3   Grease and line the slow cooker with baking paper. Gently place pate brisee creating the edges with your hands. Pour the squash mixture over and flatten the surface with a spatula.

4   Cook on low setting for 4 hours. Turn off the cooker and allow it to stand for 30 minutes.

5   Now gently remove the pie from the cooker and transfer to a serving platter. Refrigerate overnight and serve.

Make It Different

Classic squash pie is always a good option to make in your slow cooker. Its nice cinnamon taste is definitely something everybody will enjoy. However, if you have time, you can easily turn this classic recipe into a real pleasure. I wanted to share this amazing pecan and chocolate topping recipe. It tastes so amazing and gives your pie an entirely new dimension of flavors. Give it a try on the next page!

Pecan Topping

7oz of pecans
3 tbsp of whipping cream
2 tbsp of butter, melted
3 tbsp of granulated sugar
1 tsp of lemon zest 1 tsp of freshly ground chili pepper
1 tsp of salt

Chocolate Topping

7 oz cooking chocolate
3 tbsp whipping cream
1 tsp vanilla extract

Preparation

1   Melt the butter over medium-high heat. Add sugar and stir well until caramelized. Now add lemon zest, whipping cream, and pecans. Cook briefly, for 2-3 minutes and remove from the heat. Pour the mixture gently over the pie.

2   Now you should melt the chocolate. The easiest way to do this is to place it in a microwave for two minutes. Transfer to a small pot and heat up over medium heat. Add whipping cream and vanilla extract. Give it a good stir and remove from the heat. Use to top your pie. Refrigerate overnight and serve.

Make Your Own Pate Brisee

If you're in a hurry, frozen pate brisee is really a great option. But, if you have some extra time, you can easily make your own pate brisee. For a perfect pate brisee you will need:

Ingredients

2 cups of all-purpose flour
3 tbsp of butter, melted
½ cup of cold water
1 tbsp of sugar
½ tsp of salt

Pate Brisee Preparation

1   Whisk the ingredients together with electric mixer on high. Divide mixture into two equal pieces. Spread some more flour on your working surface and gently form ½ inch thick discs. Wrap tightly each disc with a plastic wrap and refrigerate for about one hour before use.

2   Pate brisee can stay in the freezer for a couple of weeks.

Crème Brûlée

 **5** Minutes    **2** Hours    **4** Servings

About Crème Brûlée

I wanted to demystify a famous restaurant-style crème brûlée. It takes only five ingredients to prepare this lovely French dessert and with just a few tricks, you can even prepare it in your slow cooker. It's really not that difficult but this simple recipe will make you a kitchen hero. The soft heavy cream is the 'creme' in this amazing dessert. Add some egg yolks to bind the ingredients together, vanilla bean for lovely taste, and amaze everyone with your culinary skills.

Nutritional Information

KCAL	PRT	CARB	FATS
226	14g	19g	9g

Ingredients

5 cups of heavy cream
8 egg yolks
1 cup of sugar plus 4 tbsp for topping
1 vanilla bean, split lengthwise
¼ tsp of salt

Preparation

1 In a large bowl, combine heavy cream with egg yolks and sugar. Beat well with an electric mixer on high. Using a sharp knife, scrape the seeds out of your vanilla bean and add them to your heavy cream mixture. I like to use the remaining of my vanilla bean. Finely chop it and add to the mixture. This, however, is optional. You can also add one teaspoon of pure vanilla extract for some extra flavor.

2 Now whisk in salt and beat well again. Pour the mixture into four standard-sized ramekins. Set aside. Take 4 x 12" long pieces of aluminum foil and roll them up. You want to get snake-shaped pieces of the aluminum foil. Curl each piece into a circle, pinching the ends together. Place in the bottom of your slow cooker. Place each ramekin on aluminum circle and pour enough boiling water to reach up to about 1/3 of the way.

3 Close the cooker's lid and set the heat to low. Cook for two hours, or until the crust is all set. Remove from the slow cooker and add one tablespoon of sugar in each ramekin. Burn evenly with a culinary torch until brown. Chill well and serve.

Did You Know?

Crème brûlée is also known as Trinity cream, crema Catalana, or burnt cream. It is a worldwide known dessert made of a rich custard and a top layer of caramel. The custard base is usually made with vanilla, but different restaurants serve other flavors. You can also experiment with this. Add some cherry, strawberry, or lemon extract for different versions of crème brûlée.

Crème brûlée goes back to 1691 when it was first mentioned in "Cuisinier royal et bourgeois" cookbook. In 1740 it gets confused with crème à l'Angloise (English cream) and it disappears from French cookbooks until the 1980s when it becomes extremely popular again.

Fig Spread Dessert

 **15** Minutes

 **2-3** Hours

 **16** Servings

About Fig Spread Dessert

This tasty fig spread dessert is a traditional delicacy of southern regions of Balkans. It is usually made with homemade fig spread. These lovely, balls can stand in the refrigerator up to one month which makes them perfect for when you don't feel like preparing something new. Besides, fig spread is proven to help with a sore throat, bronchitis, and colds.

Nutritional Information

KCAL	PRT	CARB	FATS
253	2g	30.6g	14.2g

Ingredients

1 cup of vegetable oil
1 cup of milk
1 cup of lukewarm water
½ cup of fig spread
1 ½ cup of all-purpose flour
½ cup of wheat groats
½ cup of corn flour
2 tsp of baking powder

Topping

2 cups of brown sugar
2 cups of water
½ cup of fig spread

Preparation

1. First, you will have to prepare the topping because it has to chill well before using it. Place sugar, fig spread, and water in a heavy-bottomed pot. Bring it to a boil over medium-high heat and cook for 5 minutes, stirring constantly. Remove from the heat and cool well.

2. In another pot, combine oil with lukewarm water, milk, and the fig spread. Bring it to a boil and then add flour, wheat groats, corn flour, and baking powder. Give it a good stir and mix well continue to cook for 3-4 more minutes. Chill well and form the dough.

3. Using your hands shape 2 inches thick balls. This mixture should give you about 16 balls, depending on the size you want. Gently flatten the surface and transfer to a lightly greased slow cooker. Cook for 30 minutes on high, then reduce the heat to low and continue to cook for two more hours.

4. Remove from the slow cooker and pour the cold topping over them. Refrigerate for about an hour and serve.

How to Prepare a Homemade Fig Spread

Homemade fig spread is a classic Mediterranean treat. Besides being a great dessert, this extremely easy to make spread is perfect for a sore throat, coughing, bronchitis, and colds. For this purpose, heat up one tablespoon of fig spread in a microwave and use instead of regular syrups. For this amazing, spread you will need:

Ingredients

2 lbs of fresh figs, peeled and chopped
3.5 oz brown sugar
3.5 oz coconut nectar
1 lemon, juiced
Water

Preparation

1   Place sugar and coconut nectar in a deep pot and add enough water to cover it. Bring it to a boil and add figs and lemon juice. Reduce the heat to minimum, cover, and cook for about an hour, stirring occasionally.

2   Remove from the heat and cool. Pour the fig spread in glass jars with a tight lid. Keep in the refrigerator.

Greek Cheesecake

 **15** Minutes  **2** Hours  **8** Servings

About Greek Cheesecake

The slow cooker's cheesecake? Sounds difficult, I know. But the preparation is not that different than any other, typical cheesecake recipe. This decadent, Greek inspired, creamy cheesecake with luxurious cranberry topping is absolutely amazing and a perfect addition to a fancy dinner party or a family reunion. Having that said, it's time to give this famous dessert a try.

Nutritional Information

KCAL	PRT	CARB	FATS
322	14.2g	57.8g	4.5g

Ingredients

2 lbs Greek yogurt
2 cups of sugar
4 eggs
2 tsp lemon zest
1 tsp lemon extract
½ tsp salt
1 cheesecake crust

Topping

7 oz dried cranberries
2 tbsp cranberry jam
2 tsp lemon zest
1 tsp vanilla sugar
1 tsp cranberry extract
¾ cup lukewarm water

Preparation

1 Preheat oven to 350 degrees.

2 In a large bowl, combine together Greek yogurt, sugar, eggs, lemon zest, lemon extract, and salt. Using an electric mixer, beat well on low until combined.

3 Grease a medium-sized spring form pan with some oil. Place crust in it and pour in the filling. Flatten the surface with a spatula. Leave in the refrigerator for about 30 minutes.

4 Meanwhile, prepare the topping. Combine cranberries with cranberry jam, lemon zest, vanilla sugar, cranberry extract, and water in a small pan. Bring it to a boil and simmer for 15 minutes over medium-low heat. You can add one teaspoon of cornstarch, but this is optional.

5 Fill your slow cooker with 1/2 inch of water and position a rack in the bottom. Set the cheesecake on the rack and top with cranberries. Cover the slow cooker with a triple layer of paper towels and the lid. Turn the cooker to high and cook for 2 hours without peeking. Turn off the heat and let stand until the slow cooker has cooled, 1 hour.

6 Run a sharp knife around the edge of your cheesecake. Refrigerate overnight.

Did You Know?

This worldwide popular dessert actually comes from ancient Greece. The earliest mention of this creamy recipe is in the book on the art of making cheesecakes by the Greek physician Aegimus. After the Roman conquest of Greece, the recipe spread throughout the ancient Rome and slowly gained its popularity.

A modern recipe we all know was developed in 1872 by William Lawrence from Chester, New York. He was trying to recreate a French cheese Neufchâtel, when he accidentally came up with an idea "unripened cheese" that is heavier and creamier.

Today, there are several different basic cheesecake recipes, depending on the type of cheese used for the creamy filling. In the United States and Canada, all recipes use cream cheese; in Italy, ricotta cheesecake is more popular than the American cream cheesecake; while in Germany, Netherlands, and Poland, most of the recipes use quark.

How to Make Your Own Cheesecake Crust

If you're in a hurry, a store-bought cheesecake crust will do the job. However, if you do have some time to spare and want to create your own, homemade, crust, I have a perfect recipe that will complete the taste of this lovely Greek-inspired cranberry cheesecake. You will need:

Ingredients

1 ½ cup butter, softened
1 cup granulated sugar
1 egg, separated
¼ cup honey
1 tbsp ground ginger
1 tsp bicarbonate of soda
2 cups all-purpose flour

Preparation

1   In a large bowl, combine one cup of butter, ½ cup of sugar, egg white, and honey. Beat well with an electric mixer on low. Now add ground ginger, bicarbonate of soda, egg yolk, and flour. Continue to beat until completely incorporated. Using your hands, shape the dough and place on a lightly floured surface. Roll out until about 0.5 inches thick.

2   Spread some parchment paper over a baking sheet and place the dough in it. Bake for 15 minutes, remove from the oven and cool for a while. Transfer to a food processor or a powerful blender and mix for 20-30 seconds. Transfer to a bowl. Now add the remaining butter and sugar. Mix well and use as the base of your cheesecake.

Warm Winter Compote

 **5 Minutes**

 **6-8 Hours**

 **8 Servings**

About Warm Winter Compote

Cooked fruits, cinnamon, and cloves – a perfect combination for a lovely winter dessert. The thick fruit liquid with this amazing aroma will simply warm your heart on a cold day and fill you up with some great nutrients. I like to add the smallest amount of rum in this recipe, but that's up to you. With or without it, warm winter compote will bring smiles on everyone's faces.

Nutritional Information

KCAL	PRT	CARB	FATS
385	3.1g	100g	1.1g

Ingredients

1 lb fresh figs
7 oz Turkish figs
7 oz fresh cherries
7 oz plums
3.5 oz raisins
3 large apples
3 tbsp of cornstarch
1 tsp of cinnamon, ground
1 tbsp of cloves
1 cup of sugar
1 lemon, juiced
3 cups of water

Preparation

1   Simply combine the ingredients in a slow cooker and pour 3-4 cups of water (depending on how much liquid you wish.

2   Close the lid and set the heat to low. Cook for 6-8 hours.

Did You Know?

The compote is a French word for 'mixture', but the term was derived from the Latin word 'compositus' which also means a mixture. It goes back to the medieval Europe when it was made with different fruits, sugar syrup, and spices. It came up with a believe that fruits prepared like this effect the humidity of the body and was mostly prepared as a medicine. However, the amazing taste was too appealing which is exactly why it soon gained its popularity as a dessert. The old believes were soon forgotten and compote gained its place at the tables throughout the entire Europe. In the Mediterranean region, compote is traditionally based on fresh figs, dates, and plums. The options and combinations are endless and it is totally up to you to choose your favorite one.

CHAPTER TEN

7-Day Meal Plan
with Shopping Guide

The slow cooker is truly a perfect investment if you're looking for a nice hot meal when you get home from work. However, slow cooker also means hours and hours of cooking, usually larger quantities of food. And it's quite logical – when you're about to spend 6-8 (or even more) hours preparing food, you probably won't be interested in getting one serving of soup or stew. It would be time wasting and not very economic. This is exactly why I have chosen meals that will taste the same, or even better, the day after. With carefully chosen recipes, leftovers can become quite handy and you won't have to think about every single meal during a day and let's be honest, most of us really don't have time for that. I have created a one-week meal plan that works perfectly with leftovers and has everything covered, from breakfast, snacks, to lunch, and dinner. Braised Swiss Chard, Spinach Pie, Mushroom Kebab, and especially Greek dolmades will definitely taste better when left in the refrigerator overnight (even for a couple of days). Next to the meal plan you will also find a shopping list that will help you to get ready. Use your slow cooker to make your life easier, healthier, tastier, and to get the most out of Mediterranean cuisine!

Save Time with Your Slow Cooker!

Monday

Breakfast: Eggplant Moussaka, page 56-59
2 slices of bread
Snack: Warm Winter Compote, page 154-155
Lunch: Spring Spinach Soup, page 40-41
Spinach Pie, page 74-77
Snack: Warm Winter Compote, page 154-155
Dinner: Mercimek, page 34-35
Calories: 1413

Tuesday

Breakfast: Mushroom Kebab, page 98-99
2 slices of bread
Snack: Apple Pie, page 136-139
Lunch: Mercimek, page 34-35
Meat Pie with Yogurt, page 108-109
Snack: Warm Winter Compote, page 154-155
Dinner: Sour Zucchini Stew, page 72-73
2 slices of bread
Calories: 1583

Wednesday

Breakfast: Spinach Pie, page 74-77
fresh lemonade
Snack: Apple Pie, page 136-139
Lunch: Chicken Vegetable Stew, page 92-93
Snack: Greek Cheesecake, page 150-153
Dinner: Stuffed Onions, page 126-127
2 slices of bread
Calories: 1587

Thursday

Breakfast: Patlican Kebab, page 66-69
fresh orange juice
Snack: Greek Cheesecake, page 150-153
Lunch: Vegetarian Paella, page 78-79
Snack: Crème Brûlée, page 144-145
Dinner: Vegetarian Paella, page 78-79
Calories: 1597

Friday

Breakfast: Cold Cauliflower Salad, page 52-53
3 slices of bread
Snack: Warm Winter Compote, page 154-155
Lunch: Pumpkin Soup, page 38-39
Roast Lamb, page 116-117
Snack: Greek Dolmades, page 62-63
Dinner: Creamy Leblebi Stew, page 54-55
Crème Brûlée, page 144-145
Calories: 1657

Saturday

Breakfast: Greek Dolmades, page 62-63
2 slices of bread
fresh orange juice
Snack: Cold Cauliflower Salad, page 52-53
2 slices of bread
Lunch: Braised Swiss Chard, page 50-51
2 slices of bread
Snack: Pumpkin Soup, page 38-39
Dinner: Moussaka, page 110-111
Greek Dolmades, page 62-63
Calories: 1504

Sunday

Breakfast: Stuffed Peppers, page 128-129
2 slices of bread
fresh orange juice
Snack: Braised Swiss Chard, page 50-51
2 slices of bread
Lunch: Chopped Veal Kebab, page 104-105
Snack: Stuffed Collard Greens, page 122-125
Dinner: Pumpkin Soup, page 38-39
Chopped Veal Kebab, page 104-105
Calories: 1644

Meat

Lamb Shoulder, 1 lb
Lean Veal Meat, 1 lb
Chicken Breast, 1 lb
Lean Ground Beef, 5 ½ lbs
Whole Chicken, 3 lbs
Veal Shoulder, 2 lbs

Vegetables

Eggplants, 5 lbs
Tomatoes, 8 medium-sized pcs.
Spinach 1 lb (12 oz)
Onions, 2 lbs
Carrots, 8 medium-sized pcs.
Zucchini, 5 medium-sized pcs.
Red Bell Peppers, 3 pcs.
Swiss Chard, 1 lb
Broccoli, 1 lb (10 oz)
Cauliflower, 1 lb (7 oz)
Potatoes, 3 medium-sized pcs.
Green Bell Peppers, 2 pcs.
Fire Roasted Tomatoes, 12 oz
Pumpkin, 2 lbs
Green Peppers, 2 lbs
Collard Greens, 1 ½ lbs
Wine Leaves, 40 pcs.

Fruit

Figs, 1 lb
Turkish Figs, 7 oz
Cherries, 7 oz
Plums, 7 oz
Raisins, 3 ½ oz
Apples 2 ½ oz
Lemons, 2 pcs.
Dried Cranberries, 7 oz

Legumes

Red Lentils, 8 oz
Yellow Wax Beans, 2 oz
Green Peas, 4 oz
Chickpeas, 7 oz

Dairy Products and Eggs

Mozzarella, 5 oz
Kaymak Cheese, 3 ½ oz
Eggs, 19 pcs.
Butter, 1 lb
Sour Cream, 8 oz
Liquid Yogurt, 24 fl oz
Mascarpone, 4 oz
Feta Cheese, 4 oz
Goat's Cheese, 4 oz
Milk, 1 qt. carton
Greek Yogurt, 2 lbs (8 oz)
Heavy Cream, 2 lbs
Double Cream, 4 oz

Other

Olive Oil, 1x 16 oz bottle
Vegetable Broth, 16 fl oz jar
All Purpose Flour, 1 lb
Button Mushrooms, 12 oz
Breadcrumbs, 6 oz pack
Flaxseed, 2 oz
Standard Pie Dough, 1 pack
Yufka Sheets, 1 pack
Standard Cheesecake Crust, 1 pack
Cranberry Jam, 7 oz jar
Rice, 1 ½ lbs
Pide Bread, 1 piece

Herbs and Spices

Salt, 1 pack
Black Pepper, 1 small pack
Oregano, 1 small pack
Ground Cinnamon, 1 small pack
Cloves, 1 small pack
Sugar, 2 lbs
Cumin, 1 small pack
Cayenne Pepper, 1 small pack
Celery, 3 ½ oz
Celery Root, 7 oz
Vanilla Sugar, 1 small pack
Garlic, 2 medium-sized heads
Ground Turmeric, 1 small pack
Saffron, 8 threads
Vanilla Bean, 1 piece
Rosemary, 1 small pack
Mint, 1 small pack

Conclusion

By now I hope you have realized that a slow cooker is not a myth nor something to be afraid of. It was designed to help you eat clean, tasty food, prepared in the healthiest way there possibly is. When combined with the word's best diet – the Mediterranean diet, slow cooking gets an entirely new dimension of benefits and flavors. These 50 recipes are based on fresh organic ingredients and aim to remove the slurry of chemicals and other unhealthy components often found at our table. They are also perfectly designed to show you that a slow cooking doesn't have to be boring at all – even everybody's favorite pizza will taste ten times better when prepared slowly in the old fashioned, Mediterranean way.

Make sure to try all my recipes and leave some comments. Your feedback and comments mean the world to me. Please take a moment and tell me what you think about these meals and preparation methods. Both, positive and negative feedback will challenge me to write more efficiently in the future.

Thank you for taking the time to go through this cookbook and enjoy your new way of cooking!

Wish you all the best,
Julia Garcia

Julia Garcia, creator of the popular Mediterranean recipes, is a nutritional enthusiast. Born and raised in a Spanish family, she grew up in the vibrant and exotic Mediterranean region, spending most of her time in and around the kitchen preparing traditional and authentic foods to enjoy with friends and family.

For most people living in the Mediterranean region it appears to come natural to live a healthy lifestyle, eating the right foods, loving life and maintaining a perfect body weight. This however, can be a quite difficult task for people who grew up in other regions. How can all of the above be combined with a busy work schedule? What if we don't have the same authentic foods and ingredients? How do I change my eating habits?

As Julia became older and started to travel the world for her nutritional studying, she kept hearing the same questions over and over again. There seemed to be a lot of confusion, and the Mediterranean lifestyle was considered a beautiful fairytale. Knowing that EVERYONE can achieve this lifestyle, Julia began to note down the recipes of the food she and her family were consuming every single day for the past years, and still counting today. She also asked the help of her grandmother for those special (secret) traditional recipes.

From that moment on, she is determined to share and help to educate people who are struggling with weight problems, health, and a stressful life. How come nobody in the Mediterranean region is ever stressed about anything?

Her cookbooks are written and designed for people that are struggling to achieve their weight goals, eating the right nutrients, and living a healthy lifestyle.

You will not only get to taste her family recipes, but traditional food throughout the entire Mediterranean region. As you go through her cookbooks, you will find out that there is a lot more to discover. You will be introduced to traditional recipes and cultures from countries such as Croatia, Greece, Italy, Turkey, Tunisia, and of course Spain.

Let's start living healthier, more passionate and spend more time with family and friends!

APPENDIX A

Conversion Tables

Volume Equivalents (Liquid)

US Standard	US Standard (Ounces)	Metric (Approx.)
1 tablespoon	0.5 fl. oz.	15 ml
2 tablespoons	1 fl. oz.	30 ml
¼ cup	2 fl. oz.	60 ml
½ cup	4 fl. oz.	120 ml
1 cup	8 fl. oz.	240 ml
1 ½ cups	12 fl. oz.	355 ml
2 cups or 1 pint	16 fl. oz.	475 ml
4 cups or 1 quart	32 fl. oz.	1 L
1 gallon	128 fl. oz.	4 L

Oven Temperatures (Degrees)

Fahrenheit (F)	Celsius (C) (Approx.)
275	140
300	150
325	165
350	180
375	190
400	200
425	220
450	230
475	245
500	260

Volume Equivalents (Dry)

US Standard	Metric (Approx.)
¼ teaspoon	1.25 ml
½ teaspoon	2.5 ml
¾ teaspoon	3.66 ml
1 teaspoon	5 ml
1 tablespoon	15 ml
¼ cup	60 ml
½ cup	120 ml
¾ cup	180 ml
1 cup	240 ml
2 cups or 1 pint	480 ml
3 cups	720 ml
4 cups or 1 quart	960 ml
½ gallon	2 L
1 gallon	4 L

Weight Equivalents

US Standard	Metric (Approx.)
½ ounce	14 g
1 ounce	29 g
1 ½ ounces	43 g
2 ounces	57 g
4 ounces	113 g
8 ounces	227 g
16 ounces or 1 pound	454 g
32 ounces or 2 pound	907 g

Abbreviations

Abbreviations	Measurements
C	Celsius
CAL	Calorie
CARB	Carbohydrate
F	Fahrenheit
Fl, fl, fl.	Fluid
g, g., gr, gr.	Gram
Gal, Gals., gals.	Gallon
L, L., l, l.	Liter
Lb, lb, lbs	Pound
Min	Minute
mL, ml, ml.	Milliliter
Oz, oz.	Ounce
Pers.	Person
PRT	Protein
Pt, pt, pts, pts.	Pint
Tbsp, tbsp.	Tablespoon
Tsp, tsp.	Teaspoon

Recipe Index

Index

VISIT AMAZON.COM/AUTHOR/JULIA-GARCIA TO READ EXCERPTS

66637872R00099

Made in the USA
Lexington, KY
19 August 2017